Desire Unleashed: Exploring Sex Magic for Connection and Healing

A Path to Spiritual Intimacy and Power

Erin Bennett

Table of Contents

INTRODUCTION

Welcome to "Desire Unleashed: Exploring Sex Magic for Connection and Healing - A Path to Spiritual Intimacy and Power." In this e-book, we embark on a journey of self- discovery, exploring the profound connection between sexuality, spirituality, and personal growth.

Sex magic, a practice that combines sexual energy with intention and ritual, has been used for centuries across cultures to tap into the transformative power within us. This ancient art offers a unique path to deepening intimacy, healing emotional wounds, and unlocking personal power.

Throughout this book, we will delve into the essence of sex magic, shedding light on its history, dispelling misconceptions, and unveiling its potential for connection and healing. We will examine how sexual energy can be harnessed and channeled for personal and spiritual transformation.

Chapter by chapter, we will explore various aspects of sex magic. We will learn practical techniques for cultivating and harnessing sexual energy, enhancing sensitivity, and awakening the mind-body connection. We will uncover rituals and practices that invite profound emotional and energetic connection with ourselves and our partners, creating sacred spaces for exploration and growth.

Moreover, we will delve into the healing potential of sex magic, addressing the impact of sexual trauma and offering techniques to release emotional blocks and trauma through the power of sexual energy. We will also explore the spiritual dimension of sex magic, delving into transcendent experiences, connecting with higher consciousness, and using this practice for personal empowerment and spiritual growth.

As we journey together, we will also tackle important ethical considerations, emphasizing the importance of consent, communication, and boundaries in sex magic practices. We will discuss how to navigate challenges and establish a safe and respectful space for exploration.

Finally, we will explore how to integrate sex magic into our daily lives, finding ways to bring this transformative practice into our relationships, creative pursuits, and personal goals.
Through "Desire Unleashed: Exploring Sex Magic for Connection and Healing - A Path to Spiritual Intimacy and Power," you will discover the incredible potential of sex magic to ignite passion, deepen connection, and unlock your true spiritual and personal potential. Embrace this journey of self-discovery and empowerment as we embark on a path of healing, intimacy, and personal growth.

CHAPTER I

Understanding Sex Magic

What is sex magic?

Sex magic, a term that resonates with both intrigue and controversy, represents a unique fusion of sexuality, spirituality, and magical practice. Rooted in ancient traditions, this esoteric art has endured through the ages, captivating the minds of seekers and challenging societal norms. This essay explores sex magic, delving into its historical origins, the diverse approaches that various cultures and mystical traditions have taken, and the contemporary interpretations that continue to shape this enigmatic practice.

The roots of sex magic extend deep into the annals of human history, finding expression in the sacred rites of historical societies. In societies like ancient Greece, Egypt, and India, the intertwining of sexuality and spirituality was not merely a taboo but a revered practice. In Egypt, the myth of Osiris and Isis symbolized the divine union that mirrored the cyclical nature of life, death, and rebirth. The sacred mysteries of Eleusis in Greece celebrated the holy marriage between Demeter and Persephone, embodying the cycles of fertility and growth.

In India, the Tantric traditions viewed sexual energy as a potent force for spiritual awakening. Tantric rituals, deeply rooted in Hinduism and Buddhism, sought to harmonize the dualities within the individual by exploring the union of Shiva and Shakti, the masculine and feminine energies. Sexuality was considered a path to transcendence, a means of attaining higher states of consciousness and realizing the interconnectedness of all things.

As the Middle Ages unfolded, the alchemical tradition introduced the concept of the "alchemical marriage" — a symbolic union of opposites to achieve spiritual transformation. Alchemists, engaged in the pursuit of transmuting base metals into gold, drew parallels between their material endeavors and the inner alchemy of the soul. Sexuality, regarded as a microcosm of the cosmic dance, became a metaphor for the mystical union of polarities within the alchemist.

Secret societies and mystical orders of the Middle Ages, such as the Knights Templar, were rumored to engage in secretive practices involving sex magic. While historical accuracy is often elusive, these legends contribute to the mystique surrounding the practice, hinting at the esoteric nature of the union between sexuality and spirituality during this period.

During the Renaissance and Enlightenment periods, they witnessed a resurgence of interest in mystical and occult practices. Figures like Paracelsus and John Dee incorporated alchemical and magical principles into their pursuits, contributing to the revival of ancient mystical traditions. The Hermetic tradition, emphasizing the interconnectedness of the spiritual and material realms, paved the way for the exploration of sex magic in the Western esoteric tradition.

In the 19th century, the spiritualist movement and the Theosophical Society delved into the mystical aspects of sexuality, drawing inspiration from Eastern philosophies. Helena Blavatsky and other Theosophists explored the idea of sexual energy as a means of tapping into higher dimensions of consciousness. This period set the stage for the influential role that sex magic would play in the subsequent occult revival of the 20th century.

At the forefront of the 20th-century occult revival stands Aleister Crowley, a central figure synonymous with the revival and modernization of sex magic in the Western esoteric tradition. Crowley, influenced by various mystical traditions, including Tantra and Western occultism, incorporated sex magic into his philosophical system known as Thelema. Thelema, with its central tenet "Do what thou wilt shall be the whole of the Law," underscored the importance of individual will and the pursuit of personal enlightenment.

Crowley's rituals, such as the Gnostic Mass and the Rites of Eleusis, involved sexual acts as a means of consecrating and elevating the magical experience. The use of sexual energy, according to Crowley, could unlock hidden potentials and propel practitioners toward spiritual ascent. While Crowley's approach to sex magic was provocative and controversial, it left an indelible mark on the Western esoteric tradition, influencing subsequent generations of occultists and magicians.

Parallel to Crowley's endeavors, the exploration of Tantra in the Western world gained momentum. Influential figures like Sir John Woodroffe (Arthur Avalon) introduced Tantric concepts to a Western audience. Tantra, emphasizing the integration of sexual and spiritual energies, resonated with those seeking a holistic approach to personal transformation.

In the latter half of the 20th century, we witnessed the 1960s and 1970s counterculture movements embracing alternative spiritual practices, including those involving sexuality. The Sexual Revolution, coupled with an increasing interest in Eastern philosophies, contributed to mainstreaming ideas that had once been confined to the realms of the esoteric and mystical.
In contemporary society, sex magic remains a niche and often misunderstood phenomenon. Modern practitioners draw inspiration from ancient traditions, the teachings of Crowley, and Eastern mystical traditions, seeking to explore the transformative potential of sexual energy.
The emphasis is on consensual, intentional practices that foster personal empowerment and spiritual growth.

Contemporary sex magic rituals may involve meditation, visualization, and symbolic gestures, creating a sacred space for participants to connect with higher states of consciousness. Ethical considerations, such as consent and clear communication, are paramount, reflecting a heightened awareness of power dynamics and the potential for misunderstanding within the practice.

Despite its rich historical and cultural roots, sex magic remains shrouded in misconceptions and taboos that have endured through the ages. Cultural and religious conditioning, sensationalism in popular culture, and the influence of patriarchal norms have contributed to the stigmatization of sex magic as deviant or sacrilegious. The association with secretive societies and the shadowy allure depicted in media often obscures the practice's genuine spiritual and transformative aspects.

To dispel these shadows, a nuanced understanding of sex magic is essential. Acknowledging its historical roots and cultural diversity allows for a more comprehensive perspective. Challenging ingrained cultural and religious conditioning requires a reassessment of societal attitudes toward sexuality and spirituality. By addressing gender dynamics, practitioners can move towards a more inclusive and empowering representation of sex magic. Moreover, countering the sensationalism perpetuated by popular culture demands discernment and a critical examination of media portrayals. Education becomes a powerful tool in demystifying sex magic, allowing individuals to differentiate between authentic representations and sensationalized dramatizations. Ethical concerns within the practice should be openly discussed, emphasizing the importance of transparency, communication, and establishing clear boundaries.

In conclusion, sex magic, a mystical practice that intertwines the intimate with the spiritual, weaves a narrative through the ages, traversing ancient civilizations, esoteric traditions, and contemporary occult revivals. From the sacred unions of antiquity to the provocative rituals of Crowley and the inclusive perspectives of modern practitioners, sex magic invites individuals to explore the depths of their desires and the mysteries of existence.

As society continues to evolve, the shadows surrounding sex magic beckon to be dispelled. In unraveling the secrets of this esoteric practice, we confront our biases, challenge societal norms, and embrace the profound and transformative potential of the union between sexuality and spirituality. The journey into sex magic is not merely an exploration of the physical and metaphysical realms but a voyage into the innermost recesses of the human spirit.

Historical and cultural perspectives on sex magic

Sex magic, a practice that intertwines sexuality with spirituality and the mystical, is a tapestry woven through the fabric of human history and diverse cultures. From the sacred rites of ancient civilizations to the esoteric teachings of renowned occultists, the historical and cultural perspectives on sex magic offer a fascinating journey into the intricate connections between the physical and the metaphysical. This essay explores the roots, evolution, and cultural nuances surrounding sex magic, tracing its threads through the epochs of time.

To understand sex magic, we must first peer into the sacred rituals of ancient civilizations, where the union of sexuality and spirituality was not merely accepted but revered. In ancient Egypt, the myth of Osiris and Isis symbolized the divine union that mirrored the cyclical nature of life and death. Sexuality, far from a taboo, was celebrated as a cosmic dance, an integral part of the natural order. The sacred mysteries of Eleusis in ancient Greece similarly embraced the divine union, emphasizing the cycles of fertility, growth, and renewal through the mythic marriage of Demeter and Persephone.

In the mystic traditions of ancient India, Tantra emerged as a profound exploration of the interplay between sexuality and spirituality. Tantric practices viewed the human body as a microcosm of the universe, and sexual energy was considered a potent force that could be directed toward spiritual awakening. The union of Shiva and Shakti, representing the masculine and feminine energies, was a central theme in Tantra, symbolizing the cosmic dance of creation and dissolution.

The quest to transmute base metals into gold mirrored the alchemical processes within the soul. Alchemists sought not only material transformation but also spiritual enlightenment, and sexuality became a metaphor for the union of opposites within the individual. The alchemical marriage, a symbolic union of masculine and feminine principles, embodied the mystical union sought by practitioners.

Secret societies, such as the Knights Templar, further added to the mystique surrounding sex magic during the Middle Ages. Whispers of their secretive rituals, including the alleged worship of the idol Baphomet and engagement in sacred unions, added intrigue and speculation. Though historical accuracy remains elusive, these legends contribute to the enigmatic aura surrounding sex magic during this period.

During the Renaissance and Enlightenment periods, they witnessed a resurgence of interest in mystical and occult practices. Figures like Paracelsus and John Dee integrated alchemical and magical principles into their pursuits, contributing to the revival of ancient mystical traditions. The Hermetic tradition, emphasizing the interconnectedness of the spiritual and material realms, opened pathways for the exploration of sex magic within the Western esoteric tradition.

In the 19th century, the spiritualist movement and the Theosophical Society further fueled the interest in esoteric knowledge. Helena Blavatsky and other Theosophists delved into the mystical aspects of sexuality, viewing it as a means of tapping into higher dimensions of consciousness. This period set the stage for the influential role that sex magic would play in the subsequent occult revival of the 20th century.

At the forefront of the 20th-century occult revival stands

Aleister Crowley, a central figure synonymous with the revival and modernization of sex magic in the Western esoteric tradition. Crowley, influenced by various mystical traditions, including Tantra and Western occultism, incorporated sex magic into his philosophical system known as Thelema. Thelema, with its central tenet "Do what thou wilt shall be the whole of the Law," underscored the importance of individual will and the pursuit of personal enlightenment.

Crowley's rituals, such as the Gnostic Mass and the Rites

of Eleusis, involved sexual acts as a means of consecrating and elevating the magical experience. The use of sexual energy, according to Crowley, could unlock hidden potentials and propel practitioners toward spiritual ascent. While Crowley's approach to sex magic was provocative and controversial, it left an indelible mark on the Western esoteric tradition, influencing subsequent generations of occultists and magicians.

Parallel to Crowley's endeavors, the exploration of Tantra

in the Western world gained momentum. Influential figures like Sir John Woodroffe (Arthur Avalon) introduced Tantric concepts to a Western audience. Tantra, emphasizing the integration of sexual and spiritual energies, resonated with those seeking a holistic approach to personal transformation.

In the latter half of the 20th century, we witnessed the

1960s and 1970s counterculture movements embracing alternative spiritual practices, including those involving sexuality. The Sexual Revolution, coupled with an increasing interest in Eastern philosophies, contributed to mainstreaming ideas that had once been confined to the realms of the esoteric and mystical.

In contemporary society, sex magic remains a niche and often misunderstood phenomenon. Modern practitioners draw inspiration from ancient traditions, the teachings of Crowley, and Eastern mystical traditions, seeking to explore the transformative potential of sexual energy. The emphasis is on consensual, intentional practices that foster personal empowerment and spiritual growth.

Contemporary sex magic rituals may involve meditation, visualization, and symbolic gestures, creating a sacred space for participants to connect with higher states of consciousness. Ethical considerations, such as consent and clear communication, are paramount, reflecting a heightened awareness of power dynamics and the potential for misunderstanding within the practice.

Despite its rich historical and cultural roots, sex magic remains shrouded in misconceptions and taboos that have endured through the ages. Cultural and religious conditioning, sensationalism in popular culture, and the influence of patriarchal norms have contributed to the stigmatization of sex magic as deviant or sacrilegious. The association with secretive societies and the shadowy allure depicted in media often obscures the practice's genuine spiritual and transformative aspects.

To dispel these shadows, a nuanced understanding of sex magic is essential. Acknowledging its historical roots and cultural diversity allows for a more comprehensive perspective. Challenging ingrained cultural and religious conditioning requires a reassessment of societal attitudes toward sexuality and spirituality. By addressing gender dynamics, practitioners can move towards a more inclusive and empowering representation of sex magic.

Moreover, countering the sensationalism perpetuated by popular culture demands discernment and a critical examination of media portrayals. Education becomes a powerful tool in demystifying sex magic, allowing individuals to differentiate between authentic representations and sensationalized dramatizations. Ethical concerns within the practice should be openly discussed, emphasizing the importance of transparency, communication, and establishing clear boundaries.

In conclusion, sex magic is a phenomenon that

transcends time and cultural boundaries, weaving threads through the epochs of human history. From the sacred unions of antiquity to the provocative rituals of Crowley and the inclusive perspectives of modern practitioners, sex magic invites individuals to explore the depths of their desires and the mysteries of existence.

As society continues to evolve, the shadows surrounding

sex magic beckon to be dispelled. In unraveling the secrets of this esoteric practice, we confront our biases, challenge societal norms, and embrace the profound and transformative potential of the union between sexuality and spirituality. The journey into sex magic is not merely an exploration of the physical and metaphysical realms but a voyage into the innermost recesses of the human spirit. It is a tapestry of desire, woven with threads that connect us to the cosmic dance of creation and the enduring quest for transcendence.

The connection between sex, energy, and spirituality

The intricate interplay between sex, energy, and spirituality has been a subject of fascination, reverence, and contemplation across diverse cultures and throughout the epochs of human history. This paper explores the profound relationship between these three elements, tracing the threads woven through ancient traditions, mystical practices, and contemporary perspectives. From the sacred rites of ancient civilizations to the esoteric teachings of spiritual traditions and modern explorations of consciousness, exploring the union between sex, energy, and spirituality reveals a complex and deeply ingrained aspect of the human experience.

In ancient civilizations, the recognition of sexuality as a cosmic force manifested in sacred rituals and religious practices. Ancient Egypt, with its myths of Osiris and Isis, exemplified the divine union as a cosmic dance, mirroring the cyclical nature of life, death, and rebirth. Sexuality was not seen as a mere physical act but as a sacred expression of cosmic principles, ensuring the land's fertility and the community's prosperity.

Similarly, in ancient Greece, the mysteries of Eleusis celebrated the sacred marriage between Demeter and Persephone, embodying the cycles of fertility and growth. The intertwining of sexuality with the divine underscored the belief that the physical act held spiritual significance, connecting individuals to the rhythms of the natural world and the mysteries of creation.

The Tantric traditions of India offer a profound exploration of the integration of sex and spirituality. Tantra, rooted in both Hinduism and Buddhism, views sexual energy as a potent force for spiritual awakening. The union of Shiva and Shakti, representing the masculine and feminine energies, symbolizes the cosmic dance that underlies all of creation. Tantric rituals and practices aim to harness and elevate sexual energy, guiding practitioners toward higher states of consciousness and self-realization.

In Tantric philosophy, the human body is considered a microcosm of the universe, and the union of opposites within the individual mirrors the cosmic dance of creation and dissolution. The deliberate engagement with sexual energy becomes a means of transcending dualities and experiencing the divine unity that lies at the core of existence.

The Middle Ages witnessed the emergence of alchemy, where the quest for the transmutation of base metals into gold became a symbolic journey of spiritual transformation. Alchemists sought not only material wealth but also the illumination of the soul. The alchemical marriage, a symbolic union of opposing elements, became a central theme, representing the integration of the masculine and feminine aspects within the individual.

Hidden within the symbolism of alchemical texts were

profound teachings about the transformative power of sexual energy. The mystical marriage symbolized the alchemical process within the soul, where the fusion of opposites resulted in the emergence of a more refined and spiritually awakened self.

During the Renaissance and Enlightenment periods, they

witnessed a resurgence of interest in mystical and occult practices. The Hermetic tradition, emphasizing the interconnectedness of the spiritual and material realms, provided a fertile ground for exploring the mysterious aspects of sexuality. Figures like Paracelsus and John Dee incorporated alchemical and magical principles into their pursuits, contributing to the revival of ancient mystical traditions.

In this era, the idea that sexual energy could be

harnessed for spiritual purposes gained prominence. The exploration of the inner realms, guided by the principles of alchemy and Hermeticism, invited individuals to recognize the transformative potential within the union of sex, energy, and spirituality.

The 19th century they witnessed the rise of spiritualism

and the establishment of the Theosophical Society, which delved into the mystical dimensions of sexuality. Helena Blavatsky and other Theosophists explored the idea of sexual energy as a means of tapping into higher dimensions of consciousness. Theosophy proposed a holistic understanding of the human being, recognizing the physical, mental, and spiritual interconnectedness.

Exploring sex, energy, and spirituality during this period broadened the acceptance of diverse spiritual perspectives. As individuals sought to understand the hidden dimensions of existence, the connection between sexuality and spiritual awakening gained renewed attention.

The 20th century marked a pivotal moment in exploring sex, energy, and spirituality with the emergence of influential occultist Aleister Crowley. Crowley's system of Thelema incorporated sex magic as a central element, emphasizing the conscious utilization of sexual energy to reach higher consciousness levels. The Book of the Law, a foundational text for Thelemites, declared, "Do what thou shall be the whole of the Law," highlighting the significance of a person's free will and the quest for enlightenment.

Crowley's provocative rituals, such as the Gnostic Mass and the Rites of Eleusis, involved sexual acts as a means of consecrating and elevating the magical experience. While controversial, Crowley's contributions left an indelible mark on the Western esoteric tradition, influencing subsequent generations of occultists and magicians.

Parallel to Crowley's legacy, the latter half of the 20th century witnessed the integration of Eastern spiritual practices into Western perspectives. The 1960s and 70s counterculture movements embraced alternative spiritualities, including those involving sexuality. With its emphasis on the sacred union of energies, Tantra gained popularity as individuals sought a holistic approach to personal transformation.

In contemporary society, exploring the connection between sex, energy, and spirituality has expanded into various spiritual and self-help movements. The concept of sacred sexuality, influenced by ancient traditions and modern reinterpretations, emphasizes the spiritual dimensions of intimate connections. Practitioners explore ways to cultivate and channel sexual energy for personal and collective healing, transformation, and spiritual evolution.

Tantric practices continue to thrive within traditional

Eastern contexts and Western adaptations. The emphasis on conscious sexuality, mindfulness, and the elevation of sexual energy aligns with a broader cultural shift towards holistic well-being and the integration of mind, body, and spirit.

Moreover, the fields of psychology and neuroscience have

begun to explore the neurobiological aspects of sexual energy and its potential impact on mental and emotional well-being. Research on the neurochemistry of sexual arousal and the role of oxytocin, the "love hormone," suggests that there may be physiological mechanisms underlying the profound emotional and spiritual experiences associated with sexual intimacy.

As exploring the connection between sex, energy, and spirituality evolves, ethical considerations become increasingly relevant. The potential for misuse or manipulation within intimate settings demands careful reflection on the ethical boundaries of practices that involve the intentional use of sexual energy. Consent, communication, and ethical conduct are crucial elements in creating a safe and sacred space for individuals engaged in spiritual and sexual exploration.

The intersection of desire and responsibility within the

realm of sex, energy, and spirituality necessitates ongoing dialogue and the establishment of ethical guidelines. Practitioners and communities engaged in these explorations are challenged to balance the pursuit of personal empowerment with a commitment to transparent communication and the well-being of all participants.

In conclusion, the connection between sex, energy, and spirituality is a profound and multifaceted exploration that spans the breadth of human history and transcends cultural boundaries. From the sacred dances of ancient civilizations to the alchemical unions of the Middle Ages, the mystical teachings of Tantra, and the provocative rituals of Crowley, the religious tapestry woven by the interplay of these elements invites individuals to explore the depths of their desires and the mysteries of existence.

As contemporary perspectives evolve, the intersection of sex, energy, and spirituality beckons individuals to embark on a personal journey of self-discovery and transformation. The ethical considerations accompanying these explorations emphasize the importance of conscious and responsible engagement with the powerful forces at play.

Ultimately, the connection between sex, energy, and spirituality acts as a prompt for the great oneness inherent in the human experience. It invites individuals to recognize the sacred dimensions of their intimate connections, fostering a holistic understanding that goes beyond the material and explores the domains of the metaphysical. As we navigate the complexities of desire, energy, and spirit, we contribute to an ongoing dialogue that seeks to unravel the mysteries of the sacred dance within the human soul.

Common misconceptions and taboos surrounding sex magic

Sex magic, a mystical practice entwining sexuality with spirituality and magical rituals, remains shrouded in misconceptions and taboos that have lingered throughout history. The very nature of combining intimate acts with mystical pursuits invites scrutiny, skepticism, and misinterpretation. This essay aims to dissect and dispel some of the common misconceptions and taboos surrounding sex magic, unraveling the shadows that obscure a nuanced understanding of this esoteric practice. By exploring the origins of these misconceptions and delving into the ethical considerations within sex magic, we endeavor to foster a more informed and open- minded perspective.

The roots of misconceptions and taboos surrounding sex magic can be traced to deeply ingrained cultural and religious beliefs that shape societal norms and values. Throughout history, various cultures have harbored anxieties about the intersection of sex and spirituality, viewing sexuality as a realm that should be kept separate from sacred or religious practices. This divide often stems from cultural perceptions of the body, pleasure, and the holy, creating an atmosphere of discomfort and secrecy around the topic.

In many religious traditions, the association of sexuality with sin or impurity has contributed to the stigmatization of practices that intertwine sex and spirituality. Puritanical views, especially prevalent in Western societies, have historically cast a shadow over the exploration of sexuality in spiritual contexts. This deep-seated conditioning has seeped into the collective consciousness, perpetuating misconceptions about sex magic and labeling it as deviant or sacrilegious.

Another layer of misconception surrounding sex magic is rooted in gender dynamics and the pervasive influence of patriarchy. Historical power imbalances have often cast women as the passive recipients or conduits of male energy in traditional sex magic practices. This skewed representation has perpetuated harmful stereotypes and reinforced gender inequalities, contributing to the marginalization of women within the esoteric realms.

The association of sex magic with male-dominated occult societies and figures, such as Aleister Crowley, has further fueled the misconception that sex magic is primarily a tool for male empowerment. This imbalance not only misrepresents the diverse range of practitioners but also reinforces societal prejudices about the role of women in spiritual and magical practices. Dispelling these misconceptions requires a reassessment of gender dynamics within the context of sex magic, acknowledging and honoring the variety of viewpoints and life experiences.

The mysterious and taboo allure often attracts

sensationalism in popular culture. Media portrayals, whether in literature, films, or sensationalized documentaries, tend to exaggerate and distort the nature of sex magic for dramatic effect. This sensationalism not only perpetuates misconceptions but also contributes to the commodification of esoteric practices for entertainment purposes.
The tendency to depict sex magic as a dark and secretive art, fraught with danger and hostility, only serves to heighten public fascination and fear. While some works may strive for authenticity, many succumb to the temptation of embellishment, distorting the true essence of sex magic and perpetuating a cycle of misinformation.

Amidst the misconceptions, it is essential to acknowledge

that sex magic, like any spiritual or magical practice, is not immune to ethical concerns. The potential for misuse or manipulation within the context of intimate rituals demands careful consideration and ethical guidelines. Critics rightfully raise concerns about the blurred lines between consensual, sacred practices and exploitative behavior.

The power dynamics inherent in intimate settings,

coupled with the esoteric nature of sex magic, create a vulnerable space that can be exploited if ethical boundaries are not clearly defined and respected. Unscrupulous individuals may use the mystique of sex magic to manipulate and coerce participants, violating the principles of consent and spiritual autonomy. Navigating the ethical terrain of sex magic requires a commitment to transparency, communication, and a shared understanding of the purpose and boundaries of the ritual.

Dispelling common misconceptions and taboos surrounding sex magic necessitates a comprehensive understanding of its historical, cultural, and ethical dimensions. Education emerges as a crucial tool for demystifying this esoteric practice and fostering a more informed discourse.

Firstly, acknowledging the diverse cultural roots of sex magic, from ancient civilizations to contemporary occult traditions, allows for a more nuanced understanding of its multifaceted nature. By tracing the historical threads that weave through different cultures, one can appreciate the rich tapestry of beliefs and practices that have contributed to the development of sex magic.

Secondly, challenging ingrained cultural and religious conditioning requires a willingness to reassess preconceived notions about sexuality and spirituality. Embracing a more inclusive and open-minded perspective allows for recognizing the validity of diverse spiritual expressions, including those that involve the conscious integration of sexuality.

Thirdly, addressing gender dynamics within the realm of sex magic is imperative for dispelling misconceptions. Recognizing and amplifying the voices of women and marginalized genders in esoteric practices helps break down stereotypes and fosters a more inclusive and empowering environment.
Fourthly, confronting the sensationalism perpetuated by popular culture demands discernment and critical thinking. Encouraging media literacy and discernment allows individuals to differentiate between authentic representations of sex magic and sensationalized portrayals designed for entertainment value.

Lastly, addressing the ethical concerns associated with sex magic requires a commitment to transparent communication and the establishment of clear boundaries. Practitioners must prioritize consent, safety, and ethical conduct within the rituals, fostering an environment of trust and respect.

Sex magic, a practice that weaves together the intimate and the mystical, stands at the intersection of history, culture, and spirituality. Dispelling common misconceptions and taboos surrounding sex magic requires a multifaceted approach that embraces education, critical thinking, and ethical considerations. We can foster a more enlightened and inclusive understanding of this ancient and esoteric practice by unraveling the shadows that obscure its true nature. As society continues to evolve, the exploration of sex magic beckons us to confront our biases, challenge societal norms, and embrace the profound and transformative potential of the union between sexuality and spirituality.

CHAPTER II
Harnessing Sexual Energy

The power of sexual energy and its role in manifestation

An facet of human existence that is both fascinating and frequently misunderstood is the importance of sexual energy and the function it plays in the process of manifestation. The energy of our libido is intricately interwoven with the energy of our life force. When it is consciously harnessed, it has the potential to be a powerful force that can help us create and realize our wishes.

The sexual energy that we all possess is a fundamental power that is present inside us. The creative energy is the driving force behind procreation, but it extends far further than that. A tremendous force that can be channeled and directed towards different elements of our lives, including our goals, dreams, and aspirations, it is possible to apply this force in various ways. We can make our goals come true and bring about positive change in our lives when we actively tap into this energy and use it to our advantage.

When it comes down to it, sexual energy is the energy of life force. Our interests, aspirations, and the vigor to live our lives to the fullest are all fueled by the same energy that gives us the ability to live. When we participate in sexual action, this energy is ignited and circulates throughout our bodies, causing our senses to be stimulated and reawakening our desires. A powerful force that can be utilized for personal development, spiritual connection, and manifestation is the power of the universe.

It is one of the most important elements of sexual energy that it can go beyond the realm of the physical and connect us to something more significant. The act of engaging in sexual activity causes us to feel a profound sense of connection with our partners as well as a heightened state of awareness during the encounter. Besides being a physical link, this relationship is also energetic and spiritual. When we are in this state of profound connection and heightened awareness, we can access the power of sexual energy for manifestation. A process involving bringing our desires into existence is called manifestation. The process aligns our thoughts, beliefs, and behaviors with what we want to bring into our lives. Because it is a potent source of energy and intention, sexual energy has the potential to constitute a key component of this process. We infuse the energy of sexual activity with our wants and send it out into the universe when we participate in sexual action with a specific aim or desire in mind.

The application of sexual energy for manifestation can be accomplished in several ways. The practice of sex magic is one of the most well-known techniques. This ceremonial activity is known as "sex magic," and it involves combining sexual energy with intention to bring about particular results. It is characterized by the act of participating in sexual action while concentrating on a certain desire or objective simultaneously. The practitioners think that they can increase the process of manifestation by directing sexual energy into the desired goal.

In the realm of sex magic, the orgasm is regarded as a potent catalyst for the manifestation of desires. During an orgasmic experience, it is believed that the energy that is generated is at its highest point. If this energy is channeled with intention, it has the potential to significantly impact the manifestation process. The goal of practitioners of orgasm is to increase the possibility of their objectives being realized by sending a focused burst of energy and intention out into the cosmos. This is accomplished by concentrating on the desired outcome while they are experiencing an orgasmic experience.

However, it is essential to keep in mind that sex magic is not the only method that may be utilized to cultivate sexual energy for manifestation. There are a variety of additional ways in which sexual energy can be employed, including through the practices of meditation, breathwork, and visualization. The most important thing is to actively direct our sexual energy toward our desires while simultaneously cultivating awareness and intention surrounding our sexual energy.

There is a common misunderstanding regarding the power of sexual energy and manifestation, which is that it is only focused on acquiring material possessions or satisfying superficial needs. While it is true that sexual energy can be utilized to attract material riches, it can also be directed toward other elements of our lives, such as personal development, healing, and spiritual connection. Sexual energy can be useful in attracting money abundance. You can direct sexual energy toward any aspect of your life that you would like to improve or modify. Sexual energy is a power that is both adaptable and diverse.

The notion that sexual energy is intrinsically lusty or wicked is yet another common misunderstanding. Sexual energy is indeed connected to our most basic wants; nevertheless, sexual energy is neither intrinsically good nor unhealthy. Regarding how it is channeled and directed, it is a neutral energy that may be utilized for either beneficial or negative ends, depending on the circumstances. Sexual energy can be potent for personal development, spiritual connection, and manifestation- related activities provided it is utilized mindfully and respectfully.

In conclusion, the power of sexual energy in manifestation is a fascinating component of the human experience that we have. When we can harness sexual energy consciously and intentionally, it has the potential to be a powerful force that can help us create and actualize our wishes. Whether it be through practices like as sex magic or other methods of harnessing sexual energy, we have the potential to tap into this potent life force and use it to bring our dreams and aspirations into reality. This is something that we can do. Unlocking the transforming potential of our sexual energy and bringing about positive change in our life can be accomplished via the cultivation of awareness, intention, and respect surrounding our sexual energy.

Techniques for cultivating and harnessing sexual energy

Understanding the relationship between the physical and spiritual components of human existence is one of the key principles that must be understood to have the ability to harness sexual energy. Practitioners of Eastern philosophies such as Tantra and Taoism hold the belief that sexual energy is a potent life force that is capable of being altered and enhanced. Techniques such as controlling one's breath, meditating, and being conscious of one's surroundings are extremely important in channeling this energy.

The purposeful manipulation of breathing patterns during intimate times is meant by the term "breath control," which is frequently linked with Tantric ceremonies. People can improve their awareness of sensations and redirect the flow of sexual energy throughout the body by slowing down and deepening their breath. This is a practice that individuals can engage in. This method not only amplifies the pleasure that is experienced, but it also helps to cultivate a more profound connection between partners. In Taoist practices, a similar emphasis is placed on the regulation of one's breath, to circulate sexual energy through the Microcosmic Orbit, which is a channel connecting various energy centers in the body.

One more effective method for harnessing sexual energy is through the practice of meditation. Individuals can cultivate better self-awareness and control over their desires via mindfulness. Through meditation, one can examine their thoughts and sensations without being attached to them or passing judgment on them. This opens up a place for the deliberate redirection of sexual energy. A more balanced and harmonious relationship with one's sexuality can be achieved via the practice of mindfulness, which can be incorporated into one's daily life.

Psychotherapy and contemporary psychiatric techniques, which are rooted in Western traditions, also recognize the significance of comprehending and utilizing sexual energy. Although Napoleon Hill is credited with popularizing the idea of sexual transmutation in his book "Think and Grow Rich," the concept argues that refocusing one's sexual energy on creative endeavors and personal growth can result in enhanced productivity and success. This concept is consistent with the thought that sexual energy, when actively harnessed, can serve as a source of motivation for personal development and accomplishment.

Through the combination of physical postures (asanas), breath control (pranayama), and meditation, yogic practices provide a holistic approach to cultivating sexual energy. Practitioners of Kundalini Yoga concentrate on reawakening the dormant energy located at the base of the spine and directing it upward through the chakras and other energy centers. This transforming process not only adds to an increased sense of vitality and well-being but also helps develop one's spiritual consciousness. Through the combination of physical movement and awareness of the breath, individuals can harness sexual energy to achieve both physical and spiritual benefits.

Meditation and the ability to control one's breath are only two aspects of the role of mindfulness; it also includes the ability to be fully present during intimate moments. By encouraging individuals to engage in sexual acts with full awareness, mindful sexuality urges individuals to let go of the conditioning and expectations that society has placed on them. Through the cultivation of a more profound connection between partners, mindful sexuality has the potential to result in relationships that are more rewarding and satisfying.

For successful cultivation of sexual energy, it is vital to investigate the emotional elements of sexual energy. The process of recognizing and expressing feelings that are associated with sexuality can help release energy that has been repressed and contribute to a more positive relationship with one's wants. There is a positive and open attitude toward sexual energy that may be fostered via the use of psychotherapeutic treatments such as sex therapy. These approaches equip people and couples with the tools necessary to negotiate the emotional obstacles that are associated with sexuality.

Partner-based techniques, in addition to individual activities, have the potential to strengthen the connection between the two of you and the shared experience of sexual energy. Tantra, which originates in ancient Indian practices, emphasizes the coexistence of male and feminine energies. Couples can generate a harmonic flow of sexual energy between them by engaging in rituals, practicing communication exercises, and breathing in synchronization with one another. This not only strengthens the closeness of the connection between the two of you, but it also encourages emotional closeness and mutual comprehension.

An endeavor that involves the cultivation and harnessing of sexual energy is a journey that spans not only the physical but also the mental and emotional components. Various approaches of comprehending and harnessing this powerful life energy can be found by utilizing techniques derived from both Eastern and Western traditions. Whether through the control of one's breath, meditation, mindfulness, or practices involving a partner, individuals can start on a transforming journey that extends beyond the realm of merely experiencing physical pleasure. It is possible to experience more vitality, healthier relationships, and a deeper connection to the profound force of sexual energy if one incorporates these strategies into their day-to-day existence. The adoption of a holistic approach to sexuality can not only help to an individual's well-being, but it can also contribute to a life that is more satisfying and harmonious.

Practices for increasing sensitivity and arousal

In the field of human sexuality, sensitivity and arousal play important roles since they have an impact on the quality of intimate experiences as well as the general well-being of an individual. A significant number of people are looking for strategies to improve these areas of their sexuality to ensure that their intimate life is more rewarding and satisfying. The purpose of this essay is to investigate a variety of techniques that attempt to increase sensitivity and arousal. These practices will be derived from traditional knowledge and modern approaches. Understanding and appreciating these practices can lead to a more profound connection with one's body and a heightened sensation of pleasure. These practices range from mindfulness techniques to physical exercises.

The practice of mindfulness, which has its origins in ancient Eastern philosophies such as Buddhism, has recently garnered a lot of attention in the field of sexual health and wellness. People can heighten their sensitivity to touch, taste, smell, and other sensory stimuli by bringing their conscious awareness to the present moment throughout their meditation practice. Through the practice of mindful sexuality, one can establish a more profound connection with the physical and emotional components of arousal by concentrating on the sensations that occur within the body without passing judgment on them. By engaging in activities such as mindful breathing and body scanning, individuals can enhance their sensitivity, so setting the way for a sexual encounter that is more in line with their desires and more joyful.

Tantric techniques, which have their roots in Buddhist and Hindu traditions, provide a holistic approach to sexual sensitivity and arousal with their holistic approach. Tantra is a spiritual practice that emphasizes mind, body, and spirit interdependence. It views sexual energy as a potent force that can be utilized for spiritual development. Tantric rites and exercises, such as the Heart Salutation and Eye Gazing, help cultivate a profound connection between couples, increasing their sensitivity to the wants of one another that they share. Tantra facilitates a deeper feeling of arousal by building a deliberate and sacred place for intimacy. This allows the practice to go beyond the strictly physical and incorporate pleasure's emotional and spiritual elements.

A significant impact on sensitivity and arousal can be achieved by practicing breathwork techniques, such as those in yoga and tantra programs. In addition to oxygenating the body, deep, rhythmic breathing also assists in releasing tension and is associated with improving general awareness. By slowing down the tempo and improving the connection between couples, controlling one's breath during intimate moments can heighten arousal and increase the intensity of the experience. Through the deliberate concentration on breath, individuals can access their sensual rhythms, which in turn helps them develop a more profound comprehension of their bodies and wants.

Increasing sensitivity can be accomplished straightforwardly and practically by exploring erogenous zones. It is general knowledge that erogenous zones are located in the vaginal region; nevertheless, they can be found anywhere on the body. Individuals can discover new sources of pleasure by focusing on locations such as the neck, ears, inner thighs, and even regions that are not immediately noticeable. As a result of the wide range of preferences and sensitivities that exist between couples, open communication is necessary for this inquiry. It is possible to have a more complex and heightened experience of arousal if one takes the time to comprehend and traverse these zones.

In conversations regarding sexual sensitivity and arousal, physical exercise is frequently disregarded as an irrelevant topic. In addition to being beneficial to one's general health, regular physical activity directly impacts one's sexual well-being. When it comes to arousal, cardiovascular activity, in particular, is helpful since it stimulates blood circulation, which is vital. The benefits of strength training include increased stamina and flexibility, which in turn contribute to a more varied and satisfying sexual life. In addition, yoga and other mindful movement practices can enhance body awareness, facilitating a more profound connection between individuals and the feelings they experience in their bodies.

This can be accomplished by the utilization of sensory aids, such as sexual books, films, or art, which can stimulate the imagination and contribute to increased sensitivity. Engaging with various forms of erotica can serve as a source of inspiration and fresh ideas for intimate moments. Nevertheless, it is of the utmost importance to approach such materials with mindfulness, ensuring they are by one's beliefs and boundaries. Sensual aids have the potential to be solid instruments for heightening arousal and igniting creativity; nevertheless, their utilization must be done so in a consensual manner and with due regard for the comfort levels of the individual.

One of the most time-honored methods for enhancing sensitivity and arousal is massage, which can be performed either by providing or receiving. The power of touch is enormous, and massage enables partners to explore each other's bodies in a loving and delightful way. A Swedish or aromatherapy massage are two examples of techniques that not only soothe the body but also heighten the body's sensitivity to sensation. It is possible to create a more personal and indulgent encounter by incorporating sensuous oils or lotions into the event. This will add a layer of sensory stimulation.

It is vital to investigate various forms of touch to be aware of one's and partner's bodies. It is possible to discover new pathways to pleasure by experimenting with soft caresses, gentle strokes, or more assertive touches. Communication is of the utmost importance in this investigation because every individual has their own preferences and thresholds for stimulation. To build a shared space for finding and improving sensitivity, partners might construct a space by freely stating their wants and boundaries.

The importance of emotional connection cannot be stressed when it comes to the pursuit of increased sensitivity and arousal. Trust, vulnerability, and a profound emotional connection are the building blocks that provide the groundwork for experiences that are profoundly intimate and gratifying. By engaging in communication that is both open and honest about desires, fantasies, and boundaries, partners can create an atmosphere in which they feel secure to explore and express themselves within the relationship. An environment conducive to the natural development of sensitivity and arousal is created when couples engage in emotional intimacy, strengthening their overall connection.

Practices for developing sensitivity and arousal offer a variety of approaches, spanning from ancient traditions to modern-day exercises. These practices are part of the broader landscape of human sexuality, characterized by its diversity. Collectively, the practices of mindfulness, tantra, breathwork, exploration of erogenous zones, physical activity, sensual aids, massage, varied touch, and emotional connection all contribute to a sexual experience that is more rewarding and fuller. Adopting a communicative and open-minded approach is necessary to incorporate these practices into one's life successfully. This approach must also acknowledge the singularity of one's preferences and wishes. People can engage on a journey toward a more sensual, rewarding, and comprehensive experience of sexuality by building a deeper connection with their bodies and fostering emotional intimacy with a partner. People can pursue this path.

Exploring the mind-body connection in sex magic

Throughout human history, sex magic—a mystical and esoteric discipline that combines spirituality and sexuality —has captivated and mystified people. Sex magic, which has its roots in antiquated customs and is supported by several occult movements, is the practice of using the powerful energy of sexual excitement for magical or spiritual purposes. Understanding the mind- body connection, which holds that the fusion of mental and physical energy can result in profoundly transformational experiences, is fundamental to this practice. We examine how the mind-body connection is used to channel and direct sexual energy for spiritual development, personal transformation, and the manifestation of desires as we delve into the complexities of sex magic in this section.

Understanding that sexual energy is a powerful force that can be used for both pleasure and spiritual uplift is the foundation of sex magic. Ancient cultures, including Western occult traditions such as the Hermetic Order of the Golden Dawn and some components of Hindu Tantra, acknowledged the transformational power of sexual energy. These traditions view the mind-body link as a holy bridge that can lead to higher states of awareness and magical manifestations when deliberately explored.

Originating in ancient Indian traditions, tantric rituals provide insights into the relationship between the mind and body in sex magic. Tantra practitioners aim to achieve spiritual enlightenment by transcending the physical act of sex, viewing sexual energy as a manifestation of divine energy. Tantric practitioners strive to guide the flow of sexual energy through the subtle energy channels called nadis or meridians by practicing mindfulness, breath control, and focused intention during sexual activities. By deliberately investigating the mind-body link, the spiritual potential that has lain dormant might be reawakened, and a union with the divine facilitated.

The idea of "sex magic" became popular in late 19th and early 20th-century Western esoteric traditions. Prominent occultists like Thelema founder Aleister Crowley were among those who incorporated sex magic into their mystical practices. Viewing sexual energy as a potent force that might be used to accomplish magical goals, Crowley placed a strong emphasis on ritual, focus, and imagery. According to Crowley's teachings, the mind was essential in forming and guiding the energetic currents created during sexual activities toward specific magical objectives.

A crucial element of the mind-body link in sex magic is visualization. When having sex, practitioners frequently visualize symbols or engage in complex mental imagery to give the act a magical quality. To achieve this process, one must imagine the desired result—a spiritual awakening, personal transformation, or the realization of a particular desire—in vivid detail. It is thought that visualization leaves a mark on the subconscious, influencing the direction of the energy released during a sexual act.

The mind-body link in sex magic requires concentration and effort. Practitioners focus their mental attention on a specific aim or desired result during sexual activity. It is believed that by focusing intently, the practitioner can align the energetic vibrations linked to sexual pleasure with their magical aim. Deepening the effectiveness of sex magic is said to require the ability to focus intensely throughout the physical act of sex.

In sex magic, ritualistic activities are essential because they provide a framework for securing the mind-body connection. Rituals offer a symbolic and structured setting where sexual activities are carried out with a deliberate and mystical goal. To improve the ritualistic experience and direct attention toward the desired magical result, additional elements like candles, incense, and specially chosen words of power may be included. Rituals create a sacred container for the transforming energies of sex magic by helping the practitioner connect to higher spiritual realms.

In sex magic, the mind-body link also entails the knowledge of and work with the chakras, which are energy centers. Many mystical traditions, such as Tantra and Kundalini Yoga, view the chakras as essential energy centers that regulate various facets of the human experience. Practitioners think they can activate and elevate these energy centers, resulting in spiritual awakening and expanded consciousness, by matching sexual energy with particular chakras. During sexual practices, consciously focusing on chakras improves the mind-body connection and helps energy flow toward spiritual goals.

In sex magic, breath control—a technique present in both Eastern and Western mystical traditions—is incorporated into the mind-body link. During intercourse, controlling one's breath consciously improves focus, awareness, and the flow of life force. To enhance the transforming power of sexual energy, practitioners try to strengthen the mind-body connection by syncing breath with the rhythm of sexual action. This deliberate breathing emphasizes the importance of breath in spiritual and magical acts and is strongly related to the idea of prana, or life force.

In sex magic, the mind-body connection goes beyond the act itself and includes integrating sexual energy into everyday life. Intentional living, mindfulness, and meditation are standard techniques among practitioners to keep their states of consciousness elevated and open to magical energies. Constant communication between the mind and body permits a continuous flow of sexual energy that can be focused on spiritual development and supernatural goal fulfillment.

It is important to remember that sex magic is a very subjective and individualized discipline with a focus on the mind-body connection. The most critical ethical factors are permission, intention, and respect for each party's autonomy. A careful and responsible approach is necessary for those who explore sex magic, understanding that the mind-body link is a precious and potent part of the human experience.

The mind-body connection is the key to mystical revelations and life-changing events in the mysterious field of sex magic. Sex magic, which has its roots in antiquated customs and is supported by several esoteric movements, is the deliberate investigation of sexual energy for the sake of transforming oneself, achieving spiritual advancement, and manifesting desires. The mind-body link is a critical concept emphasizing the sacred union of physical and mental forces through

Tantric rituals, Western occult traditions, or a synthesis of multiple mystical aspects. In the quest for spiritual advancement and magical mastery, practitioners of sex magic go through complex pathways that go beyond the realm of ordinary consciousness. They want to unravel the deep mysteries of the mind-body connection.

CHAPTER III

Rituals and Practices for Connection

Creating sacred space for sex magic rituals

Sex magic is the deliberate use of sexual energy for spiritual and magical objectives. It is a mystical technique that combines the sensual and the sacred. Establishing a sacred space, or a dedicated area where practitioners can communicate with the divine, channel transforming forces, and actualize their objectives by uniting their body, mind, and spirit, is fundamental to this esoteric practice. We discuss the significance of constructing a sacred container for sex magic rituals in this essay, looking at the symbols, rituals, and attentive practices that go into making this sacred space where these powerful experiences take place.

The first step in creating a sacred atmosphere for sex

magic rituals is realizing that the surroundings of the ritual greatly influence the energetic dynamics at work. A sex magic ritual's location is regarded as a temple, much like in other mystical traditions; it's a place where the commonplace becomes a conduit for the divine and the extraordinary rises above the ordinary. During the ritual, practitioners aim to harness transforming energies, concentrated intention, and concentration through this sacred place.

Establishing and consecrating the sacred place for sex

magic is primarily dependent on rituals. To create a visually and energetically charged setting, these rituals frequently include symbolic objects like candles, incense, and ritual implements. For instance, burning candles symbolizes the discovery of spiritual understanding, and incense's perfume might serve as a bridge to the other world. The deliberate placement of ritual implements, like athames or wands, adds to the ceremony's symbolic language and emphasizes its purpose.

In many magical traditions, especially sex magic, the ceremonial act of casting a circle is commonplace. By using ceremonial magic and Wiccan rituals, practitioners mark the sacred place with a symbolic circle that separates it from the outside world. By forming a dedicated container, this circle acts as a protection barrier, allowing the energies generated during the sex magic ritual to be directed and contained. Invoking the elemental forces, calling upon the quarters, and asking celestial presences to observe and partake in the ritual are standard practices associated with casting circles.

Creating a sacred place in sex magic involves more than just physical rituals; it also involves participants' mental and emotional preparation. Setting intentions and practicing mindfulness are essential parts of this process. To develop a focused and open mind, practitioners partake in contemplative activities like meditation. Participants match their mental and emotional energy with the intended magical consequences by setting explicit intentions for the ritual. This state of mental and emotional readiness strengthens the participants' bond with the divine and increases the sex magic ritual's overall potency.

A sex magic ritual's complex tapestry is enhanced by symbols and archetypal images, which provide the sacred area with multiple levels of interpretation and importance. Symbols like pentagrams, chalices, and unique colors are used in numerous traditions to invoke specific energies or archetypal forces. These symbols serve as entry points, bridging the spiritual and the every day and giving the subconscious mind a visual language to understand. Adding symbols to the sacred area makes the ritual more potent, and participants can access universal energies and archetypes that transcend individual consciousness.

Another prominent aspect used to create a powerful atmosphere for sex magic rituals is sacred geometry. It is said that shapes like spirals, triangles, and rounds contain specific vibrational frequencies that connect with various facets of the divine. The energetic flow within the sacred space can be enhanced by drawing geometric patterns on the floor or by incorporating sacred geometry into ritual equipment. Throughout the ceremony, these forms act as both visual and energetic focal points, directing the currents of sexual energy and intention.

A major component of sex magic is the alteration of consciousness, and materials like incense, oils, or plants are frequently used to promote an altered state. These materials may be selected based on their alignment with particular energies or deities. For example, burning herbs such as damiana or mugwort improves psychic sensitivity and sensual awareness. These materials are carefully chosen and prepared, which helps to create a sacred space and helps participants reach the elevated levels of awareness that are desired in sex magic rituals.

In sex magic rituals, music and soundscapes are effective instruments for establishing a sacred atmosphere. Certain sounds have vibrations and frequencies that can affect energetic states and improve the ritual experience. Practitioners frequently select sounds that align with the ritual's aim, whether chanting, ambient music, or rhythmic drumming. In the sacred place, the harmonious interaction of sound and sexual energy creates a transforming and immersive experience.

In sex magic rituals, deity invocations or evocations are frequently included. Participants invoke particular gods, goddesses, or archetypal energies in these rituals to witness and strengthen the ceremony. By establishing a link with the divine, these invocations bring beneficent spirits into the sacred place. Whether the objective of the ritual is for love, fertility, healing, or spiritual illumination, the choice of deities is often in line with it. The ritual is elevated above the physical act by the contact with these heavenly energies, which gives the union of sexual energy a layer of spiritual meaning.

The four classical elements—Earth, Air, Fire, and Water—

are incorporated, which enhances the sacred space's meaning. The ritual's depiction of each element promotes a peaceful and balanced atmosphere, which is linked to particular attributes and energies. Crystals or salt can represent Earth, incense or feathers can represent Air, candles or a dedicated flame can represent Fire, and a chalice or consecrated Water might represent Water. By balancing with these elemental energies, the ritual is grounded in the natural world, and the participant's connection to the more extensive web of life is strengthened.

Establishing a sacred place for sex magic rituals requires

a foundation of open communication and consent. Boundaries should be set and respected; all participants must be willing and enthusiastic. Beyond verbal consent, effective communication is also necessary for energetic consent and continuous awareness of participants' requirements and comfort zones. Establishing a holy space necessitates mutual respect and confidence to direct the energies created during the ritual toward constructive and agreeable results.

Closing the sacred place is an equally important step

when the sex magic ritual is over. This entails grounding any lingering energy, releasing the energetic circle, and expressing appreciation for the divine forces called upon. To integrate the sensations of the ritual, practitioners can spend some time introspecting, meditating, or spending intimate time together. Consciously closing the sacred place gives participants a sense of closure and completion as they return to everyday life.

Building a sacred place for rituals, including sex magic, is

a complex and multifaceted process that integrates energetic, symbolic, and physical components. Every part of the ritual, from calling upon deities and casting circles to utilizing materials, symbols, and deliberate soundscapes, helps create a sacred space in which the fusion of spirituality and sexuality can take place. In addition to providing a setting for the actual act of sexual intercourse, the sacred space is a transformational vessel through which practitioners can access the mysteries of the body, mind, and spirit. The intentional creation of a holy place becomes an essential part of the trip as people delve deeper into sex magic; it serves as a conduit for the fusion of the energies of desire and divine communion, weaving a tapestry of magic, intention, and spiritual awakening.

Incorporating intention and visualization into sexual experiences

With its physical, emotional, and spiritual facets, sexuality is a very personal and intricate part of the human experience. The intentional investigation of sexual encounters has gained popularity recently, with an emphasis on integrating intention and vision. This method recognizes that our minds greatly influence our experiences of pleasure and connection. This section explores the importance of bringing intention and vision into sexual encounters, looking at how the mind's power can improve intimacy, strengthen bonds, and lead to a more satisfying sexual life.

In the context of sexual encounters, the idea of intention refers to establishing a specific, deliberate objective for the interaction. It changes the emphasis from just enjoying oneself physically to having sex with more intention and mindfulness. Whether engaged in activities with a partner or on your own, intention offers a framework for guidance that shapes the whole experience. This goal could be anything from exploring new aspects of one's sexuality to strengthening emotional ties and encouraging closeness to being open and curious about the present moment.

In paired experiences, intention-driven sexual interactions require open communication. Partners can discuss their goals for their sexual relationship as well as their desires and boundaries honestly and openly. In addition to creating a shared understanding, this communication enables the co-creation of intents that suit the requirements and preferences of both parties. By putting objectives into words, one can include awareness in the experience and create the conditions for a more deliberate and thoughtful investigation of pleasure.

Intention and visualization go hand in hand. Visualization is forming mental pictures or situations that correspond with the desired experience. This technique makes use of the mind's ability to affect and improve the feelings and bodily experiences connected to sexual activity. Visualization may be a potent tool when it comes to breaking through mental barriers, examining fantasies, and strengthening relationships with partners. Individuals can create a mental landscape that shapes and enhances their sexual encounters by vividly visualizing desired outcomes or scenarios.

Visualization is a standard tool used by lone practitioners for self-evaluation and empowerment. This could be exploring personal fantasies or imagining situations that inspire joy or self-love. Visualization may be a very effective strategy when one uses it to help develop a healthy relationship with one's body, wants, and self-perception. Increasing self-awareness, confidence, and a favorable sexual self-image can all be attributed to this deliberate self-exploration.

Intention and imagery are a part of mindfulness, which emphasizes being present and involved in the moment, and they can be included in sexual experiences. People who practice mindfulness are more inclined to pay attention to the feelings, ideas, and sensations that surface during sexual activity. Through cultivating an accepting and nonjudgmental mindset toward these encounters, people can strengthen their connection to the present, increasing their enjoyment and contentment from the experience.

Tantric practices, which have their origins in antiquated Eastern philosophy, shed light on how to integrate intention and imagination into sexual encounters. According to tantric rituals, having intercourse is a holy and spiritual act that can lead to transcendent experiences. An essential component of Tantric rituals is intention setting, in which partners express their desires for the meeting and direct their energies toward common objectives. Through visualization, one can control the energy flow through the body's subtle channels, or nadis, strengthening bonds between couples and promoting a higher state of consciousness.

Intention and imagination can be applied to any part of the sexual journey, from arousal to climax and back. They are not just reserved for particular sexual acts. It is possible to enhance the experience and strengthen the mind-body connection by using mindful breathing techniques, frequently connected to Tantric and yogic practices. People can develop a higher level of awareness and become fully present and sensitive to their body's feelings by concentrating on their breathing.

Another method people infuse intention into their sexual experiences is through the practice of edging, which involves purposefully postponing the orgasm to lengthen the sexual experience. Edging is making the deliberate choice to investigate the plateau stage of arousal, and experience increased pleasure without instantly attaining climax. This deliberate wait allows for a deeper investigation of one's own sexual reaction and pleasure thresholds in addition to increasing anticipation and intensity.

Intention and imagery can be constructive for people dealing with problems like performance anxiety or body image problems. People can change their beliefs and develop a better relationship with their bodies and sexuality by making positive goals and using visualization exercises that encourage self-acceptance and pleasure. This deliberate thinking can improve general well-being, lessen the adverse effects of self-talk, and boost confidence.

Techniques for sexual awareness, like the Body Scan, provide a systematic way to integrate intention and imagination. The bodily Scan entails focusing on various physical areas and objectively observing sensations. By doing this, people can focus their attention on parts of their bodies linked to pleasure and arousal and increase their awareness of their bodies. People can develop a sound and intentional relationship with their bodies by adding intention into the Body Scan, which paves the way for more satisfying sexual experiences.

One inventive method to bring intention and visualization into sexual experiences is through the use of erotic literature, fantasies, or artistic expressions. Playing with things corresponding to one's dreams and wishes permits a mental investigation of pleasure. People can use their imagination to enhance their sexual experiences through various means, such as reading sensual literature, expressing fantasies with a partner, or creating artistic expressions that embody desired experiences.

Creating an altar or other sacred location just for sexual exploration is a common practice in religious sexual practices, such as those found in Tantra. The deliberate placement of ritual artifacts, candles, and symbols creates a visual depiction of the sacredness of sexuality. Environmental intentions and visualizing outcomes around the altar ground the encounter in a spiritual environment above and beyond the everyday.

Intention and imagination combined with an experience in pairs can result in a deeper emotional bond. Exercises involving joint visualization allow partners to share desires or envisage scenarios together. In addition to improving communication, this collaborative inquiry strengthens a couple's connection and understanding. Partners co-create an environment where their aspirations converge by coordinating their intents and imaginations, which promotes a sense of togetherness and shared purpose.

It is critical to understand that intention and visualization must be incorporated into sexual experiences in a consenting and communicative manner. To make sure that both parties are in agreement on the deliberate components of the sexual encounter, partners must have an open discussion about their desires, boundaries, and comfort levels. A safe and trusting atmosphere is facilitated by consent and continuous communication, which enables both parties to actively participate in the intentional and visible components of their shared sexual adventure.

To truly explore the depths of human sexuality, it is an intentional and thoughtful method to integrate intention and imagination into sexual interactions. This deliberate approach, whether used alone or with a partner, improves the general quality of sex and builds a stronger bond between the two people. The power of intention and visualization transcends cultural and temporal boundaries, from Tantric traditions to modern mindfulness practices, providing people with a path to a more meaningful and purposeful sexual life. Individuals can create a more profound tapestry of pleasure, connection, and intimacy by realizing the interplay between the mind and body and embarking on self-discovery, self-acceptance, and shared exploration.

Techniques for deepening emotional and energetic connection with a partner

A happy and long-lasting relationship is based on developing and preserving a solid emotional and energy bond with a partner. This connection is more profound than physical closeness; it includes comprehension, emotions, and a peaceful energy flow. This section will look at several methods for strengthening our emotional and energy bonds with our partners. These strategies provide routes to a deeper and more meaningful connection in romantic relationships, from mindful practices and energy exchange to effective communication and sympathetic listening.

Building stronger emotional and energy ties in a partnership requires effective communication. Intimacy and understanding are built on the capacity to listen with empathy and to communicate thoughts, feelings, and wishes freely. Active listening means paying close attention to your partner, recognizing their feelings, and intelligently answering. As a result, an environment of emotional safety promotes trust and a feeling of being understood and heard. Additionally, it might be beneficial to frame discussions favorably and encourage open communication by utilizing "I" expressions to express personal thoughts instead of assigning blame.

Empathy cultivation is another essential method for strengthening emotional bonds. Understanding and sharing another person's emotions is a necessary component of empathy. It necessitates paying attention to your partner's feelings, confirming their experiences, and extending compassion. Couples can deepen their relationship and overcome emotional distance by consciously placing themselves in each other's shoes. Establishing a more sympathetic relationship is facilitated by asking each other about their feelings, checking in regularly, and offering emotional support.

It is essential to use mindfulness techniques to strengthen emotional and energetic bonds. Being fully present in the moment is a critical component of mindfulness, which can increase awareness of and appreciation for the experiences that two people share in a relationship. Deep breathing exercises, meditation, and even easy activities like going for a mindful walk are examples of mindfulness activities that couples can do together. These exercises not only help people unwind but also provide an emotional safe zone where they may connect emotionally and better know one another's inner lives.

It is essential to investigate the language of love and affection to strengthen emotional ties. Love languages are the various ways that people express and receive love. Knowing your partner's preferred method of receiving and expressing love, be it through physical touch, acts of service, affirmations, gifts, or quality time, will help you express your feelings in ways that they will find meaningful. By expressing love to your partner in the most significant ways, you can deepen your emotional bond by understanding their love language.

Engaging in joint experiences and travels creates a feeling of community and shared memories, strengthening the emotional bond between partners. Engaging in enjoyable activities strengthens the relationship through shared struggles, triumphs, and giggles. This could be going on trips, learning a new hobby together, or even trying out different foods. Positive emotions are accumulated from shared experiences, strengthening the emotional bond and promoting greater intimacy.

A more esoteric but practical method for strengthening relationships between spouses is studying energetic connection and exchange. People who follow different spiritual and holistic traditions think energy is the essential force that ties everything together. Partners can investigate tantric techniques, in which the sharing of sexual energy is believed to facilitate the development of stronger emotional and spiritual ties. Tantra uses techniques like focused touch, eye gazing, and coordinated breathing to raise the level of energy connection between lovers.

Establishing routines in your relationship might help strengthen your bond on an energetic and emotional level. Rituals provide a partnership, a feeling of familiarity and structure, and help to create a shared story. These might be as easy as an annual custom, a weekly date night, or an early morning ritual. By establishing a framework for shared memories and experiences, rituals help to strengthen the sense of commitment between spouses and enhance their overall emotional bond.

Being vulnerable is an effective way to strengthen emotional bonds. Being open and sincere about one's emotions, desires, and anxieties is a necessary part of vulnerability. It calls for mutual trust and a readiness to open up to a partner about the most private parts of oneself. A deep sense of intimacy and emotional connection is created when both parties feel secure enough to be vulnerable. By encouraging understanding and support amongst couples, sharing vulnerabilities creates a space where both parties can experience emotional growth.

Deepening emotional and energy ties between spouses are primarily dependent on sexual closeness. Sexual intimacy entails a shared exploration of wants, fantasies, and emotional weaknesses in addition to physical pleasure. It's critical to have frank conversations about one's sexual wants and aspirations. A deeper emotional and energetic connection can be achieved through methods like mindful touch, prolonged foreplay, and discovering new facets of sexuality together. The focus is establishing a private area where partners truly feel seen, appreciated, and connected.

Gratitude expression is a straightforward but effective method for fostering emotional bonds. Continually praising and recognizing your partner's good traits, deeds, or efforts encourages an attitude of gratitude in your partnership. Gratitude strengthens the dynamic link between partners by creating a favorable emotional environment. By expressing gratitude for the small things in life, one can foster a sense of reciprocal appreciation and fortify their emotional bond.

Developing self-awareness is essential to strengthening emotional bonds in relationships. People must know their feelings, triggers, and behavioral patterns. People who better grasp themselves can better express their demands and handle conflict with more emotional intelligence. A more thoughtful and sympathetic exchange between partners is facilitated by self-awareness, which builds a stronger emotional bond.

One proactive method to strengthen emotional ties is to participate in relationship education or counseling. Getting expert advice can provide couples with the skills they need to resolve issues, enhance communication, and better understand one another. While counseling offers a safe space for addressing unsolved issues and fortifying the emotional connection, relationship education offers doable tools for fostering emotional intimacy.

Sustaining emotional ties in a partnership requires striking a healthy balance between independence and closeness. Each partner needs their place for personal development, hobbies, and self-care. When two people support one another's independence, their distinct identities can continue to develop, which makes their emotional bond more resilient and vibrant when they get together. A relationship that thrives on freedom and interdependence strikes a balance between individual demands and shared experiences.

Bringing lightheartedness and playfulness into the relationship is a playful yet effective way to strengthen emotional bonds. Laughing strengthens relationships between spouses and is a potent emotional bridge. Lighthearted interactions, inside jokes, and laughter help foster a healthy, vibrant environment that makes the relationship feel lighter and more like friendship.

A revolutionary method for strengthening emotional ties is to practice forgiveness and letting go of grudges. Resentment and holding onto grudges can damage a relationship's emotional foundation. It takes active decision-making to let go of hurt feelings and move forward to forgive. People who practice forgiveness allow the relationship to heal and regenerate, strengthening the emotional bond and making it more empathetic and robust.

Strengthening a relationship's emotional and energetic bonds requires a multidimensional strategy that includes sharing experiences, practicing mindfulness, having good conversations, and exploring private and vulnerable areas. These methods aid in developing a solid and meaningful bond that endures the test of time. Couples can build a foundation for a long-lasting and satisfying partnership by actively participating in these practices, which help to cultivate a relationship rich in emotional intelligence, understanding, and shared progress.

Exploring different types of sexual rituals and their benefits

Since the beginning of time, sexual rituals have been an essential component of human culture and expression. People of all different societies, faiths, and personal relationships have practiced these rituals. The purpose of these rituals, frequently infused with symbolism and significance, is to lay the groundwork for more profound connections, increased intimacy, and spiritual development. In the following paragraphs, we will delve into the varied landscape of sexual rituals, investigating their origins, goals, and potential benefits they bring to individuals and partnerships.

Among the many types of sexual rituals, one of the most famous types is rooted in religious or spiritual traditions. The incorporation of sexual aspects into religious practices is shared across all civilizations. This is done to establish a connection with the divine or reach a higher level of consciousness. Tantra is one example of a spiritual tradition that originated in ancient India and emphasizes the combination of sensuality and spirituality. Certain sexual practices, which are included in tantric rituals, are performed to channel sexual energy to achieve spiritual enlightenment and a harmonious union between couples.

Along the same lines, sacred sexuality rituals are carried out in certain Native American tribes as a means of paying homage to and establishing a connection with the community, the cosmos, and the natural world. The purpose of these rituals, which are steeped in symbolism and tradition, is to establish a deeper connection with the spiritual realm and to be regarded as a sacred expression of the energy associated with the life force.

Extending beyond the confines of the religious environment, some specific individuals and couples incorporate sexual rituals into their daily lives as a means of enhancing their interpersonal connections and strengthening their emotional attachments. These rituals can take many forms, from straightforward acts of communication and vulnerability to more elaborate ceremonies commemorating the special connection between partners.

The exchanging of fantasies and wishes is a typical type of personal sexual ritual that different people perform. Couples can have open and honest conversations about their most private dreams, which can provide a space for increased mutual understanding and exploration. Partners can establish a more profound sense of trust and a more meaningful emotional connection by discussing these intimate ideas, which can lead to enhanced happiness in the sexual element of their relationship.

Personal sexual rituals also include the assimilation of sensory experiences, which is another part of these rituals. When it comes to enhancing the sensory component of their connection, couples may be interested in exploring the usage of particular fragrances, textures, or settings. For example, this could involve using scented oils, using soft textiles, or even participating in activities such as blindfolding to enhance the sensory experience and establish a more profound connection between couples.

A further point of interest is that the practice of mindfulness during sexual interactions has become increasingly popular as a means of strengthening the connection between lovers. Mindful sex requires the participant to be present at the moment, concentrating on the sensations, feelings, and connections that they share with their partner. This increased awareness may result in a more meaningful and pleasurable sexual experience, which will ultimately lead to improved overall pleasure in the relationship.

It is possible to investigate sexual rituals within the context of therapeutic interventions, which extends beyond the domains of the personal and the spiritual. To assist individuals and couples in addressing difficulties in intimacy, communication, and sexual dysfunction, several sex therapists incorporate particular rituals into their sessions. A stronger sexual relationship can be fostered through the use of these therapeutic rituals, which may involve guided exercises, tactics for communication, and sensory exploration.

Participating in sexual rituals can improve communication and connection between couples, which is one of the most significant advantages of practicing these rituals. Individuals can cultivate trust, create emotional relationships, and foster a more profound knowledge of each other's desires and needs when they participate in their shared experiences. This, in turn, can contribute to a sexual connection that is more enjoyable and fulfilling for both parties involved.

A further benefit of sexual rituals is that they have the potential to foster a sense of presence and attentiveness during intimate moments. A space for connection and pleasure that extends beyond the physical parts of the act can be created via the practice of being fully present during sexual encounters. This is especially important in a world that is full of distractions and moves at a rapid pace. Mindfulness practice has the potential to result in heightened levels of satisfaction and a more profound sense of connection between partners.

Additionally, participating in sexual rituals might contribute to the overall enjoyment of a relationship or partnership. Because of the deliberate effort put into designing and engaging in these rituals, it is clear that the individual is committed to the connection and is willing to devote time and energy to developing the relationship. With this kind of commitment, the foundation of a relationship can be strengthened, which in turn makes the partnership more durable when confronted with difficulties.

Although sexual rituals can provide a multitude of advantages, it is vital to approach them with compassion and mutual consent to reap the total rewards. Talking clearly and honestly about boundaries and preferences is essential, as not all individuals or couples may find these practices appropriate or pleasant. Furthermore, it is necessary to consider cultural and religious factors to guarantee that any rituals selected are based on the individual's unique set of values and beliefs.

In conclusion, having the opportunity to engage in a variety of sexual rituals enables one to get access to a vast array of experiences that have the potential to improve one's personal, spiritual, and relational relationships. Sexual rituals have the potential to strengthen emotional attachments, cultivate mindfulness, and contribute to overall relationship happiness. These benefits can be derived from various sources, including religious traditions, personal connections, and therapeutic therapies. People and couples can start on a journey of self-discovery, connection, and fulfillment in their sexual and relational lives if they embrace these practices with open communication and mutual consent during their sexual and relational lives.

CHAPTER IV

Healing through Sex Magic

Understanding sexual trauma and its impact on intimacy

Innumerable people all over the world are impacted by sexual trauma, which is a problem that is highly widespread and frequently goes unnoticed. It is possible for the consequences of such traumatic experiences to resonate across numerous facets of a survivor's life, and one area that is deeply influenced is the area of having intimate relationships. We will investigate the complex relationship that exists between sexual trauma and intimacy in this essay, looking into the psychological, emotional, and physical ramifications that survivors may experience as a result of their experiences. The development of empathy, the provision of support, and eventually, the facilitation of the healing process depend on having a solid understanding of the mechanics of this connection.

In the context of sexual trauma, a wide range of situations are included, including sexual assault and abuse, sexual harassment, and sexual coercion. Those who have survived such a traumatic event frequently struggle with a complicated web of feelings, which may include feelings of shame, remorse, fear, and impotence. These emotions can significantly impact how they perceive themselves, their relationships, and the world in general. An individual's capacity to trust others, to have a sense of safety, and to engage in relationships that are healthy and consensual can be negatively impacted by the aftermath of sexual trauma, which can throw a long shadow in the context of intimacy.

When it comes to the psychological effects of sexual trauma on relationships, the erosion of trust is one of the most significant effects. A severe breach of trust that occurred during the traumatic event may make it difficult for survivors to trust other people, especially romantic partners. This may be the case because of the trauma they suffered. As a result of the breach of personal boundaries and the violation of permission, survivors may experience a persistent sense of vulnerability, which makes it challenging for them to emotionally open up and engage in intimate relationships without the fear of being subjected to additional harm.

Additionally, sexual trauma has the potential to alter an individual's image of their own body as well as their sexual characteristics. There is a possibility that survivors could have body dissociation or develop adverse body image disorders, which will cause them to feel alienated from their physical selves. This alienation can extend to the sphere of intimacy, making it more difficult for them to engage in sexual experiences fully or to develop a sense of familiarity with their bodies. To effectively address these difficulties, a nuanced and compassionate approach is required. This approach frequently involves therapy interventions that reestablish a healthy relationship with one's natural body.

From an emotional standpoint, those who have survived sexual trauma may struggle with a variety of conflicting feelings when it comes to intimate relationships. As a result of the tremendous impact of the trauma, survivors may have emotional numbness, which makes it difficult for them to connect with their feelings or the feelings of their partners. On the other hand, survivors may also suffer heightened emotional reactivity, which is characterized by the occurrence of specific triggers that elicit significant emotional responses. This can result in difficulty in maintaining emotional stability within intimate relationships.

When it comes to navigating the complexities of emotional intimacy, emotional intimacy can be especially tough for survivors. As a result of the fear of being vulnerable and the possibility of experiencing emotional anguish, survivors may experience the need to construct emotional barriers, which makes it challenging for them to engage in and cultivate personal interactions thoroughly. The emotional distance that one maintains serves as a coping mechanism to protect oneself from potential injury, yet it can also be detrimental to developing healthy and meaningful relationships.

The effects of sexual trauma on physical intimacy are significant, and they frequently take the form of a variety of struggles in sexual relationships. Survivors can have difficulties such as arousal disorders, pain during sexual activity, and a general intolerance to physical touch. Anxiety, hyperarousal, and the resurfacing of painful memories during intimate times are some of the causes of these challenges, which can be traced back to a complex interaction between psychological and physiological components.

Survivors and their partners need to have a solid understanding of the physical appearances that are associated with sexual trauma. To provide survivors with a secure environment to articulate their requirements and limits, it is necessary to demonstrate sensitivity, patience, and open communication. When it comes to treating the physical impact of sexual trauma on intimacy, seeking professional assistance, such as therapy and counseling, can be extremely helpful. This provides survivors with a supportive atmosphere in which they can heal and reclaim control over their bodies.

It is necessary to use a diversified strategy that takes into consideration the entire well-being of survivors to rebuild intimacy after sexual trauma successfully. Survivors can be equipped with the tools necessary to manage trauma-related symptoms and work toward regaining a sense of safety and control in their personal lives through the use of therapeutic therapies such as trauma-focused cognitive-behavioral therapy (TF-CBT) or eye movement desensitization and reprocessing (EMDR).

It is of the utmost importance to cultivate an understanding and helpful atmosphere within the context of personal relationships. Regarding the healing process, the partners of survivors play a critical role. This position requires patience, sensitivity, and a desire to learn about the complexity of sexual trauma. To establish a secure and mutually agreeable environment for intimate encounters, it is vital to have open discussions regarding limits, triggers, and mutual agreement.

In conclusion, it is essential to have an awareness of the influence that sexual trauma has on intimacy to develop a compassionate and well-informed response to the requirements of survivors. When it comes to creating a supportive environment that is conducive to recovery, the first step is to acknowledge the psychological, emotional, and physical ramifications that trauma has. Society can contribute to empowering survivors and creating healthy, consensual, and happy intimate relationships by emphasizing empathy, education, and open communication. Survivors can regain agency over their personal lives and progress toward a future distinguished by resilience and growth if they can access the appropriate resources and support. The journey toward healing is a complex and individualized process.

Using sex magic as a tool for healing and transformation

Throughout human history, sex has been entwined with spiritual rites and practices. Many civilizations have recognized the immense energy and connection that may be harnessed via sexual experiences. Sex magic is one such esoteric practice that draws upon the transforming potential of sexuality. Sex magic is a spiritual and metaphysical technique that blends sexuality, intention, and ritual to accomplish transformative and personal aims. It has its roots in mysticism and old traditions. This essay will examine the idea of "sex magic," its historical foundations, and how people are using it as a tool for self-healing and personal development today.

Sex magic is not a novel idea; its origins can be found in prehistoric societies where people believed that sexuality was a strong force that united the material and spiritual worlds. For instance, having sex was seen as a sacred ritual in ancient Egypt that may promote spiritual enlightenment, wealth, and procreation. Similarly, sexual energy is seen as a vital force that may be used for spiritual and personal development in Tantric traditions that have their roots in India. These antiquated methods serve as an inspiration for the current rebirth of interest in sex magic, which has modified and evolved the idea to fit modern spiritual viewpoints.

Sex magic is essentially the use of sexual energy and intention to bring about desired results. The practice is open to people of many belief systems because it is not inherently linked to any particular religious or spiritual tradition. Instead, it highlights the innate relationship between sexuality, individual energy, and the force of intention. Sex magic is the deliberate and focused utilization of sexual energy to bring about positive transformation rather than the act of sex per se.

The focus on intention-setting is a fundamental component of sex magic. During rituals, practitioners intentionally set goals or intentions when at a high level of sexual desire. This can be done alone or in partnership, and the purpose can be anything from more general objectives like manifesting good change in the world to more specific ones like personal empowerment and healing. It is thought that the high energy released during sexual pleasure acts as a potent catalyst to manifest these desires.

Rituals involving sex magic frequently incorporate symbolism, mindfulness, and visualization. During the ritual, practitioners may use particular symbols or pictures as focus points if they resonate with their aims. The intended result is vividly imagined by applying visualization techniques, giving the sexual energy direction and purpose. Here, mindfulness refers to maintaining complete awareness of the current moment while strengthening the bond between the material and spiritual dimensions of the encounter.

One common topic in the use of sex magic is healing.

People who have gone through sexual trauma or who battle with issues of empowerment and self-worth may use sex magic as a way to take back control of their emotions and bodies. For survivors, the deliberate and voluntary nature of sex magic rituals can be a transforming experience that helps them rethink their relationship with sexuality, let go of emotional barriers, and start a path toward self-discovery and healing.

Within the field of personal change, sex magic offers a distinctive pathway for people to discover and accept various aspects of themselves. The practice promotes self-reflection and self-awareness as practitioners explore their desires, fears, and objectives. Through the application of intention-setting in a sexual environment, people can harmonize their sexual energy with their personal development objectives, promoting a transformational approach that integrates their spiritual and physical selves.

It is crucial to remember that there is no one-size-fits-all method when it comes to the art of sex magic; it is very customized. While some practitioners may favor a more impromptu and intuitive approach, others may involve intricate rituals using particular objects and symbols. The secret is to employ sexual energy with awareness and purpose to fulfill spiritual and personal desires.

In their activities, modern sex magicians frequently stress the value of ethical issues, permission, and communication. The practice is based on consent, guaranteeing that each person freely participates in the ritual and understands the shared aims. Open communication between partners or within a community of practitioners is essential to keep a safe and encouraging atmosphere.

The impact of one's intentions on others and understanding the interdependence of all beings are fundamental ethical issues in sex magic. Practitioners are urged to make goals that advance both the more significant good and favorable results for themselves. This moral component highlights sex magic's potential as a tool for both individual and group transformation and sets it apart from simple self-indulgence.

Sex magic can strengthen a couple's bond in romantic relationships. Sex magic rituals can help to deepen the link between couples when they are performed as a couple with mutual agreement and shared aims. The heightened state of intimacy and vulnerability during these rituals can create a space for mutual growth and exploration by fostering a more excellent knowledge of one another's desires, anxieties, and goals.

Sex magic has its detractors and skeptics, yet it provides a distinctive method for healing and transformation. Some contend that the technique is outside the purview of conventional treatment procedures and lacks empirical support. Concerns about the possible misapplication of sexual energy or the possibility of propagating false ideas about sexuality can also give rise to skepticism. It is critical to approach sex magic with discernment, keeping one's boundaries and morals in mind.

In summary, the intriguing nexus of sexuality, spirituality, and human development is represented by sex magic. Trained in antiquated customs yet flexible enough to accommodate modern viewpoints, it provides a singular path for people to delve into the profound relationship between sexual energy and conscious manifestation. Sex magic encourages people to consciously and intentionally embrace the transformational potential of their sexuality, whether it is used for personal healing, empowerment, or as a tool to fortify intimate relationships. To fully reap the advantages of sex magic for healing and change, as with any spiritual practice, one must have an open mind, ethical considerations, and a clear grasp of their aims.

Techniques for releasing emotional blocks and trauma through sexual energy

With its complex relationship to emotions and the human mind, sexuality can promote significant healing. Emotional blocks and trauma might appear as obstacles to having satisfying and healthful interpersonal relationships with a substantial number of people. Nonetheless, several methods based on both contemporary therapy approaches and age-old wisdom utilize the transforming potential of sexual energy to remove trauma and emotional barriers. We will look at these methods in this essay and see how they might lead to self-discovery, healing, and a resurgence of empowerment.

Understanding the mind-body link is one of the

fundamental ideas behind using sexual energy to dissolve emotional barriers. Traumas and emotions are not just limited to the head; they are also stored in the body's tissues, impacting mental and physical health. Body-mind integration techniques aim to address this relationship, realizing that a comprehensive approach is necessary to remove emotional barriers.

Somatic experience is one such method, which is a

therapeutic approach created by Dr. Peter A. Levine. The significance of the body's physical experiences in processing and letting go of trauma is emphasized by somatic experiencing. When it comes to sexual recovery, practitioners emphasize reestablishing a connection with one's body during intimate times, which facilitates the release of repressed emotions and painful memories. Through mindfulness and body awareness, people can progressively let go of emotional barriers that might have kept them from participating in close relationships altogether.

Another effective method for facilitating the release of emotional barriers through sexual energy is breathwork. A great deal of stress is placed on the breath as a link between the physical and energetic parts of the self in many ancient traditions, such as yoga and Tantra. When having sex, people can uncover repressed emotions and establish a deeper connection with their bodies by breathing deeply and mindfully. People can release stuck energy and encourage flow by intentionally inhaling into tense or uncomfortable areas, which helps emotional blocks dissolve.

Tantra, an age-old spiritual discipline with Indian roots, provides a thorough method for releasing emotional obstacles via sexual energy. Through the deliberate channeling of sexual energy throughout the body, tantric practices cultivate a profound link between the energetic and physical realms. Tantra attempts to unleash the full power of sexual energy for healing and transformation via the integration of specialized physical practices, breathing exercises, and meditation. Tantric rituals create a holy space for intimate connection and emotional release, and they can be done alone or with a partner.

The therapeutic community has come to recognize the benefits of mindfulness meditation, which is frequently connected to Buddhist practices, in stress management and emotional well-being. When mindfulness meditation is used in the context of sexual recovery, it entails developing an impartial awareness of one's thoughts, feelings, and experiences during intimate moments. By observing and distancing oneself from painful or unpleasant ideas, this exercise makes room for the removal of emotional barriers and promotes a more positive relationship with one's sexuality.

It has been found that artistic expression—primarily via dance and movement—is a powerful aid for releasing trauma and emotional blockages. The body's inner wisdom is accessed through creative movement, and repressed emotions can be expressed. In particular, dance therapy allows people to move freely and truthfully, facilitating the flow and release of emotional energy. Dancing is a non-verbal way to express and process feelings; thus, including it in one's sexual healing path may be a therapeutic and empowering experience.

A controlled and deliberate environment for the release of emotional barriers through sexual energy can be established through the use of rituals and ceremonies. Rituals offer a framework for people to examine and alter their dynamic landscapes; cultural or spiritual traditions frequently influence them. Specific exercises, symbols, or affirmations intended to dispel negative energy and promote healing may be a part of these ceremonies. These ceremonies' objectives are critical because they create the conditions for a targeted and deliberate release of emotional barriers.

Sex therapy is a branch of modern psychology that uses a variety of approaches to treat emotional barriers and trauma related to sexual experiences. For instance, the goal of cognitive-behavioral therapy (CBT) is to recognize and question harmful sexuality-related thought patterns and attitudes. People can start to change their emotional reactions and remove obstacles that might be preventing them from having healthy sexual relationships by altering these thought habits. Examples of integrative approaches include somatic experience techniques, body-centered therapies, and mindfulness-based therapy.

When it comes to using sexual energy to eliminate emotional obstacles, partnership, and communication are essential. Mutual understanding and support are made possible when people in intimate relationships communicate honestly and openly. To create a shared place for healing and growth, couples can investigate strategies jointly. The approach is collaborative and considerate of each partner's journey since it strongly emphasizes permission, limits, and shared intentions.

Although sexual energy can be used to relieve emotional obstacles through these strategies, it is essential to approach the healing process with self-compassion and care. A person's healing journey is unique and gradual, so what works for one person might not work for another. Consulting with licensed experts, such as bodily therapists or sex therapists, can offer customized assistance and understanding according to each person's particular requirements and situation.

In summary, the process of releasing emotional barriers through sexual energy is complex and combines traditional healing methods with cutting-edge science. People can start a transforming journey towards healing and self-discovery by accepting the mind-body link, practicing mindfulness, and engaging in creative and intentional practices. Fostering an aware and compassionate relationship with one's sexuality is crucial, regardless of whether one incorporates modern therapeutic techniques or draws inspiration from ancient traditions like Tantra. People may have a deep feeling of empowerment and liberation when emotional obstacles are gradually lifted, and they may also have a revitalized potential for close relationships that recognize their wholeness.

Cultivating self-love and acceptance through sex magic practices

One area that has unrealized potential for personal development and self-discovery is sexuality, which is frequently veiled in social taboos and prejudices. Sex magic is one of the many spiritual and metaphysical techniques that utilize intention, energy, and ritual to harness the transformational power of sexuality. It is a distinctive approach. Applying sex magic with an emphasis on acceptance and self-love makes it an effective tool for developing a healthy relationship with one's libido and body. This essay will examine the foundational ideas of sex magic, go into its historical origins, and talk about how purposeful sexual practices can help people go on a path toward self-acceptance and love.

The word "sex magic," which may conjure images of mystery and intrigue, refers to an age-old esoteric practice in which the intentional use of sexual energy is employed to manifest particular intents or wishes. Sex magic is a cultural and spiritual practice that has its roots in Tantra, the Western esoteric tradition, and some pagan rituals. It acknowledges the power of sexual energy as a force that exists beyond the physical world. In the framework of developing self-acceptance and love, sex magic presents a unique method of empowerment and healing.

The idea that sexual energy is a transformational and creative force lies at the foundation of sex magic. People can access their inherent potential for self-improvement and recovery through the deliberate and purposeful manipulation of this energy. Setting specific goals, practicing awareness, and adding symbolic elements to heighten the ritual's energy and significance are standard techniques in sex magic rituals.

A thorough examination of one's desires, anxieties, and sexuality-related beliefs is the first step in the process for anyone looking to use sex magic to develop self-love and acceptance. The practice's cornerstone is self-reflection, which enables people to pinpoint areas of resistance, guilt, or self-judgment that might impede their ability to love themselves. These self-limiting ideas are transformed into affirmations of love and self-acceptance through the use of sex magic.

A crucial element of sex magic entails directing deliberate and affirming thoughts during intimate rituals. Affirmations are solid tools for retraining the subconscious mind because they are declarations of positive ideas and intentions. People can create affirmations that support a healthy and loving relationship with their bodies and sexuality and counteract negative self-perceptions in the framework of self-love and acceptance.

It is essential to include mindfulness exercises in sex

magic rituals to promote acceptance and self-love. Being mindful is letting go of distractions and passing judgment to be present in the moment. People can practice mindfulness during sexual rituals by paying attention to their breath, their sensations, and their connection to their partners or themselves. This increased awareness makes a greater sense of self-love and a deeper appreciation of one's physique possible.

Within the Tantric tradition, which honors the fusion of

sensuality and spirituality, sex magic rituals place particular emphasis on the fusion of a person's inner masculine and feminine energies. This union, frequently represented by the fusion of Shakti and Shiva forces, stands for the harmonious balance of opposites inside each individual. People can explore and integrate these energies through Tantric rituals, which can help them come to a more profound knowledge and acceptance of their inner duality.

A fundamental idea of sex magic is the hallowed or

ritualized place. Paying attention to the physical surroundings, adding items with personal meaning, and bringing reverence into the room are all necessary for creating an atmosphere supporting self-love and acceptance. Ritualized environments can act as holding rooms for life-changing encounters, giving people a secure and deliberate way to explore their sexuality.

Letting go of any residual shame or guilt related to

sexuality is a crucial part of developing self-love through sex magic. Rigid sexual norms and expectations are frequently imposed by society, which causes people to absorb criticism of their preferences or wants. To overcome these cultural influences and reclaim one's sexuality as a source of self-love and personal empowerment, sex magic can be a very effective strategy.

Within the field of sex magic, practices can be customized to each person's comfort level and tastes, whether they are done in pairs or alone. While some people use solitary rituals to achieve profound self-discovery, others might investigate the communal experience of sex magic with a partner who is both trustworthy and willing. To ensure that both parties are at ease and have similar goals, communication, and permission are crucial in partnered practices.

Through sex magic, each person's path to developing self-acceptance and love is particular and distinct. It necessitates sensitivity, a dedication to self-discovery, and a readiness to question deeply held sexuality ideas. Sex magic is a framework that helps people rethink how they relate to their bodies, accept their urges, and develop an empowerment that goes beyond the bedroom.

Many cultures have acknowledged the transformational power of sexuality in the past and have included sexual rituals in their religious and spiritual activities. For example, having intercourse was considered a sacred act with the possibility of spiritual awakening in ancient Egypt. Similarly, the old Indian classic Kama Sutra examines how spiritual connection and sensual pleasure coexist in close partnerships. These historical viewpoints emphasize the continued acceptance of sexuality as a potent catalyst for spiritual and personal development. Although sex magic dates back thousands of years, its modern comeback is a reflection of a rising understanding of the role that sexuality plays in overall health. A more sophisticated understanding of the enormous impact that sexual experiences can have on mental, emotional, and spiritual dimensions of life has been made possible by the field of sexology and the integration of sexual health into total well-being.

Within the framework of modern sexology, sex magic is consistent with holistic sexuality's tenets, which highlight the interdependence of the physical, emotional, and spiritual facets of human sexuality. Sexual therapists and sexologists acknowledge that deliberate and conscious sexual behaviors can have a good impact on people's body image, self-worth, and general well-being.

When people use sex magic to start the process of developing self-love and acceptance, it's essential to approach the practice with curiosity, openness, and self-compassion. Overcoming cultural conditioning, embracing a more liberated and honest expression of one's sexuality, and facing and releasing deeply rooted beliefs are all possible steps in the process. On this road of transformation, seeking advice from Tantra practitioners, sex therapists, or other qualified specialists can be very beneficial.

Finally, sex magic practices provide a deep and deliberate approach for people to develop acceptance and love for themselves. People can use the transformational power of sexual energy to let go of self-limiting ideas, accept their wants, and create healthy relationships with their bodies by fusing traditional wisdom with modern viewpoints. By deliberately including mindfulness, affirmations, and sacred space, sex magic transforms into a tool for self-actualization, celebration of sexuality as a natural and valuable part of the human experience, and personal empowerment.

CHAPTER V

Spiritual Intimacy and Power

Exploring the spiritual dimension of sex magic

Throughout human history, spiritual practices have been intricately linked with sexuality, which is frequently regarded as a very private and intimate component of human existence. An incredibly fascinating path in this field is the occult discipline of "sex magic," which uses sexuality as a powerful tool for spiritual development and metamorphosis. Sex magic explores the profound relationship between sexual energy, intention, and spirituality. It has roots in both traditional and contemporary mystical ideas. We shall travel to the spiritual side of sex magic in this essay, looking at its historical origins, guiding ideas, and modern manifestations.

The spiritual practice of sex magic is based on the idea that sexual energy is a potent force that transcends the material world and can affect the spiritual and metaphysical aspects of life. Although the phrase "sex magic" may conjure up images of mystery, it's crucial to understand that the practice encompasses more than just the physical act of sex. Instead, it entails using sexual energy consciously and purposefully to accomplish spiritual and transforming objectives.

Sex magic has historically been rooted in a variety of spiritual and cultural traditions. Sexual rites were revered in ancient Egypt as sacred practices with the power to bring about spiritual enlightenment, prosperity, and procreation. In a similar vein, the old Indian spiritual tradition of Tantra acknowledges the close relationship between spirituality and sexuality. Through the deliberate channeling of sexual energy, tantric practices aim to bring about enlightenment, unification, and spiritual awakening.

The idea of sex magic was popularized and formalized in

the Western esoteric tradition by individuals like Aleister Crowley. Modern occultism and ceremonial magic owe much to Crowley's investigation of the mystical and magical dimensions of sexuality. His groundbreaking book, "The Book of Lies," and the idea of the "Gnostic Mass," show how ritualistic rituals for spiritual study can incorporate sex magic.

The intentionality principle, which is the deliberate focus

of sexual energy on particular spiritual or transforming objectives, is the foundation of sex magic. Through rituals that involve setting specific objectives and concentrating their thoughts on desired results, practitioners harness the increased energy produced during sexual pleasure. It is said that this deliberate use of sexual energy can strengthen one's intentions and enable a closer relationship with the spiritual world.

The spiritual aspect of sex magic is based on the idea of

sacred sexuality. The concept of holy sexuality embraces the idea that sexual energy is a divine and creative power, in contrast to traditional conceptions that may link sex with guilt or shame. According to this viewpoint, having sex is a sacred rite that, when done with respect, intention, and permission, can promote spiritual and personal development. One of the fundamental principles of many spiritual traditions, including Tantra and certain paganism, is the acknowledgment of the sacred in the act of sexuality.

Mainly, Tantra provides a thorough framework for

investigating the spiritual aspect of sex magic. The literal translation of the word "Tantra" is "weave" or "loom," signifying the interconnected nature of the material and spiritual worlds. Tantric practices are a series of rituals, meditations, and visions meant to create a bridge between the individual and the divine by harmonizing and channeling sexual energy throughout the body. A central element in Tantric philosophy is the merging of the male and feminine energies inside oneself, commonly represented through Shiva and Shakti symbols.

In a Tantric context, sex magic focuses on developing awareness, presence, and mindfulness during sexual encounters. The deliberate bond between couples weaves together tantric sex magic, the recognition of the divine in every person, and the celebration of pleasure as a means of gaining spiritual understanding. Within this tradition, having intercourse turns into a sacred, metamorphic ritual that passes beyond the material world and grants access to higher states of awareness.

The spiritual aspect of sex magic is being expressed in new ways that are constantly evolving, taking modern viewpoints and ancient traditions as inspiration. For example, Neo-Tantra is a contemporary interpretation that combines Western ideas about spirituality and personal development with Tantric concepts. In this situation, using sex magic to explore one's spirituality, clear energetic blockages, and develop a closer bond with oneself and one's partner becomes possible.

The Law of Attraction's metaphysical philosophy and the concepts of sex magic are complementary to intentionally setting goals and focusing energy toward positive results. According to this fundamental law, one's intentions and the amount of energy they put into a project impact how it turns out. People who practice sex magic, which is based on the Law of Attraction, perform sexual rituals with the express goal of attracting desirable experiences, promoting spiritual development, and creating good changes in their lives.

The concept of energy transmutation, or the transformation of sexual energy into higher vibrational levels, is closely related to the spiritual aspect of sex magic. This idea is not exclusive to sex magic; it is present in many different magical traditions around the globe. When it comes to sex magic, sexual energy is purposefully elevated from lower chakras to higher energy centers, which promotes spiritual enlightenment and altered states of awareness.

To enhance the spiritual aspects of their intents, practitioners of sex magic frequently employ symbolism, archetypal imagery, and ritual equipment in their rituals. The ritualistic aspect of sex magic can be strengthened by the use of sacred geometry, crystals, candles, and particular incantations, which provide a focused and dedicated place for the interaction of spirituality and sexual energy. These are instruments for connecting with the divine and bringing intentions to life.

It is important to remember that practicing sex magic, especially with a partner, calls for a strong feeling of duty, ethical considerations, and open communication. To create a polite and safe environment for discussing the spiritual side of sex magic, consent, open communication, and shared intentions are essential. Relationships that accept the spiritual elements of sex magic frequently entail a mutual dedication to individual and group development.

In summary, investigating the spiritual side of sex magic reveals a wealth of historical knowledge, modern interpretations, and mystical philosophy. Sex magic, which has its roots in ancient customs and is constantly changing, allows people to connect the spiritual and material spheres of their lives. Intentionality, sacred sexuality, and the conscious investigation of the divine within are transforming journeys that practitioners of sex magic undertake, whether Tantra, the Western esoteric tradition, or contemporary metaphysical ideologies inspire them. Sex magic becomes a route to spiritual enlightenment, self-actualization, and the celebration of sexuality as an essential part of the human experience as people traverse the domains of intention-setting, energy transmutation, and ceremonial activities.

Connecting with higher consciousness and transcendent experiences

Over the ages, the quest for transcendent experiences and higher awareness has been a significant component of many nations' mystical and spiritual traditions. People use a variety of transformative techniques, such as meditation, prayer, psychedelics, or other therapies, to explore the mysteries of life and the depths of their consciousness. This section will discuss the idea of higher consciousness, look at several ways to get in touch with it, and consider how transcendent experiences might change people's lives regarding spirituality and personal development.

Higher consciousness is beyond the bounds of regular waking consciousness and is frequently referred to as a heightened state of awareness or enlarged perception. It includes a deep understanding of one's inner self, the unity of all things, and their more extraordinary, universal intellect and oneness with them. Although different spiritual traditions have different meanings of higher consciousness, all emphasize a shift in awareness beyond the ego and invite people to explore the infinite worlds of the mind and spirit.

One particularly well-known and extensively used technique for reaching higher awareness is meditation. Meditation, which has its roots in antiquated religions like Buddhism and Hinduism, entails developing silence, attention, and concentration to achieve a higher level of awareness. Through the practice, people can calm their minds and access more profound understanding, self-discovery, and a connection to the universal source of consciousness. Through contemplative practices such as transcendental or mindfulness meditation, people can travel within themselves to discover the depths of their awareness.

Various cultures have employed psychedelics, which are chemicals that change consciousness and experience, for millennia in both ceremonial and recreational contexts. Psychedelics have generated controversy in both science and society, although some see them as instruments for promoting transcendental experiences. It has been stated that certain substances, such as ayahuasca, LSD, and psilocybin-containing mushrooms, can cause states of expanded awareness, ego dissolution, and a deep sense of oneness with the universe. Psychedelics have the potential to be catalysts for spiritual discovery and transformation when used sensibly and purposefully.

Many spiritual traditions provide pathways to higher consciousness through contemplative activities. The Whirling Dervishes are ecstatic dancers in Sufi mysticism who use their dance to generate a trance-like condition in which they transcend conventional consciousness and tune into the holy. Similarly, contemplative prayer and divine union experiences are sought in Christian mysticism to raise consciousness and establish communication with God. The common thread across these traditions is the deliberate participation in rituals that transcend the mundane and encourage people to connect with the transcendent parts of their faith.

Breathwork is a powerful tool for transforming consciousness and accessing transcendent experiences. It includes a variety of techniques, including pranayama and Holotropic Breathwork. Using conscious breath control and manipulation to create altered states of awareness is known as breathwork. People can access deeper subconscious layers and clear energetic blocks and feel unified with the cosmic energies that permeate existence by concentrating on their breath. Intentional breathing modulation facilitates transformational and transcendent experiences by linking the physical and metaphysical domains.

With its breathtaking beauty and innate relationship to life cycles, nature provides a sacred setting for establishing a connection with higher consciousness. Many indigenous societies have acknowledged the spiritual value of nature throughout history, seeing it as a manifestation of the divine. By submerging oneself in the revitalizing forces of the Earth, people attempt to commune with higher consciousness through vision quests, forest bathing, or spiritual rites held in natural settings. Nature's simplicity and purity offer a setting for reflection, introspection, and the realization that one is a part of the web of life.

Near-death experiences, or NDEs, represent a distinct and frequently unplanned type of transcendent experience. NDE survivors describe a wide range of intense and life-changing experiences, such as emotions of unconditional love, seeing loved ones who have passed away, and feeling like they are merging with a transcendent light. Even though the scientific community disagrees over the nature of NDEs, those who have them often experience profound changes in perspective, heightened spiritual awareness, and a diminished fear of dying.

Through artistic expression—dance, music, visual arts, or literature—one might establish a connection with a higher awareness. When the creative process is approached authentically and with intention, people can access a source of inspiration outside their egoic minds. Artists frequently talk about states of flow, in which there is a profound sensation of connection with higher states of consciousness, and the barriers between the ego and the creative source melt. Participating in artistic endeavors transforms into a spiritual discipline, enabling people to surpass the mundane and transform the boundless into concrete manifestations.

Transcendent experiences can happen naturally and in various religious and spiritual contexts. They are not restricted to any one of these frameworks. People from different ethnic, religious, and secular backgrounds report having had mystical experiences marked by a sense of unity, timelessness, and ineffability. These encounters put traditional ideas of reality to the test and let people consider the potential of dimensions beyond the tangible and apparent.

Transcendent experiences have the transforming power to cause people to see things differently, break through self-limiting beliefs, and initiate significant human development. Such encounters frequently promote empathy, compassion, and a profound appreciation for the wonder and mystery of life by increasing one's sense of interconnectedness with others and the universe. People who have experienced transcendental states frequently talk about having a fresh perspective on life, improved intuition, and a long-lasting influence on their priorities and values.

Difficulties and disagreements surround the ideas of transcendent experiences and higher consciousness. Many of these experiences, according to skeptics, can be explained by psychological events, changed brain states, or neurobiological processes. Transcendent experiences are difficult to measure or justify objectively due to their subjective nature, which adds to the continuous controversy between mystical and scientific viewpoints.

The scientific community is working to comprehend the brain processes that underlie transcendent experiences, while seekers of higher consciousness and spirituality practitioners are delving deeper into their awareness. The search for transcendent experiences cuts beyond religious and cultural divides and reflects a common human desire to connect with something bigger than ourselves.

Investigating higher consciousness and transcendent experiences is a complex process combining traditional knowledge with modern techniques and the universal human search for purpose. People try to connect with the vast worlds of the metaphysical and transcend the confines of ordinary awareness through contemplative activities, psychedelics, meditation, or natural interactions. These experiences can profoundly arouse a sense of connectivity with the wonders of existence, develop spiritual growth, and awaken a deeper understanding of oneself. Pursuing greater understanding is an age-old and global undertaking that humanity will always undertake as it navigates the waters of awareness discovery.

The role of spirituality in deepening intimacy and connection

The pursuit of closeness and connection is a fundamental aspect of human interactions. Many find comfort and depth in exploring spirituality as a way to create meaningful connections while navigating the intricacies of human dynamics. Spirituality, frequently entwined with individual values, beliefs, and a sense of transcendence, can be crucial in helping people become more intimate with one another. This section explores the various dimensions of spirituality as a driving force behind deep connections, looking at how it affects shared values, communication, and creating a holy space in relationships.

Fundamentally, spirituality involves an individual's subjective investigation of existence's transcendent or divine facets. It is a facet of the human experience that touches on issues of meaning, purpose, and interconnectivity in addition to the concrete and logical. Regarding relationships, spirituality adds complexity beyond the emotional and physical, giving people a common area to delve into their innermost thoughts and collectively ponder life's riddles.

Any close relationship is built on communication, and spirituality significantly impacts how people relate to each other through conversation. When a couple has similar spiritual ideas, they frequently discover that these shared frameworks provide a common vocabulary for discussing important issues regarding existence, life, and meaning. The language of spirituality can help couples understand and connect better, whether they are participating in spiritual practices, having philosophical conversations, or exchanging personal observations.

Furthermore, spirituality can support constructive dispute resolution in interpersonal interactions. During difficult circumstances, realizing a greater purpose or common values derived from spiritual beliefs can provide guidance. Spiritually oriented couples frequently approach problems with forgiveness, compassion, and dedication to their and each other's personal development. Through grounding their relationship in spiritual principles, people can overcome obstacles in a way that fortifies rather than weakens their relationship.

Intimate friendships can be established and maintained within a basic framework of shared values anchored in spiritual ideas. A relationship gains coherence and unity when ideals are aligned, whether related to morals, ethics, or life goals. Spiritual values help people find an ordinary ethical compass by emphasizing love, compassion, kindness, and forgiveness. When spouses prioritize spiritual alignment, a harmonious resonance in values can improve communication and understanding between the partners.

Spirituality-based rituals and activities are essential for increasing intimacy between people. Engaging in spiritual rituals, such as group prayers, meditation sessions, or religious ceremonies, creates a space for reflection and connection. These rituals give off an air of reverence and purpose, creating a space where couples can connect spiritually, physically, and emotionally. Participating in these rituals fosters a sense of community and strengthens the notion that the relationship goes beyond the ordinary to the sacred.

The spiritual dimension also affects sexuality, an essential component of human interactions. Sexuality is viewed as a sacred and transformational element in many spiritual traditions. Sexual intimacy becomes a spiritual practice when it is approached with regard and mindfulness, enabling people to connect soulfully as well as physically.

Intimate moments can be enhanced, and making love is seen as a transcendent experience beyond simple physical pleasure when partners integrate spiritual awareness.

The idea of mindfulness, which is frequently connected to religious traditions like Buddhism, has become more prevalent in relationships and psychology. Being mindful entails developing awareness without passing judgment and being present at the moment. When used in a relationship, mindfulness enables people to give their partners their whole attention, creating a solid connection. Spiritual traditions frequently encourage couples to approach their relationship with awareness and attentiveness by incorporating mindfulness into their practices.

Together, you may pursue personal and spiritual development as part of your relationship's spiritual journey. When a couple sets out on a joint path of self-discovery to better understand who they are and how they relate to the divine, they frequently discover that this investigation of themselves enriches their relationship. Through spiritual growth and development in tandem, couples can enhance their closeness by attending workshops, reading and reflecting together, or going on spiritual retreats.

While spirituality plays a significant role in strengthening connections, it's essential to understand that having different spiritual beliefs can sometimes cause problems. It takes open communication, respect, and readiness to comprehend and value one another's viewpoints to navigate different spiritual pathways. Couples can regard differences as chances for mutual development and enrichment rather than barriers. Relationships that are interfaith or spiritually mixed, when handled with honesty and respect, can offer a unique forum for embracing variety and delving into the depths of different spiritual traditions.

In summary, spirituality is a potent catalyst for increasing closeness and connection in interpersonal interactions. The spiritual dimension adds layers of depth and meaning to the human experience of connection, whether through standard spiritual practices, shared values, or cooperative efforts toward personal development. When two people intentionally incorporate spirituality into their relationship, they frequently discover that it gives them a common language for communication, a moral and ethical compass, and a deep sense of togetherness that goes beyond everyday experience. People can experience a transforming and transcendent connection that transcends the physical and emotional domains when they set out to integrate their spiritual journeys.

Using sex magic for personal empowerment and spiritual growth

Throughout history, sexuality has been revered and examined in a variety of ways as a powerful force entwined with human existence. The esoteric discipline of "sex magic," where sexuality is used as a transforming instrument for spiritual development and personal empowerment, is one fascinating direction this investigation takes. Sex magic, which has its roots in antiquated customs and is now popular among mystics, encourages people to intentionally and consciously channel sexual energy to maximize its potential for spiritual growth, self-actualization, and empowerment. This section will discuss the fundamentals of sex magic, look at its background, and consider how people might use it as a means of achieving spiritual growth and self-actualization.

The understanding that sexual energy is a potent and creative force is the foundation of sex magic. This technique, which has its roots in old-fashioned esoteric traditions, recognizes the notion that the energy released during sexual stimulation is capable of profound transformation and goes beyond simple physical pleasure. Sex magic elevates sexuality to a higher, spiritual realm and celebrates its divine nature, in contrast to conventional ideas that frequently link sex with shame or repression.

Sex magic has historical roots in several cultures, including Western esoteric traditions, ancient Egypt, and India. The god Osiris was linked to sexuality's capacity for regeneration in ancient Egyptian mythology, connecting sexual rituals to rebirth both physically and spiritually. Similar to this, Indian Tantra emphasizes the merging of one's own male and feminine energies by incorporating sexual practices into a complete spiritual journey. The Western esoteric tradition's Aleister Crowley was a crucial figure in formalizing the concepts of sex magic, defining rituals and practices that aimed to channel sexual energy for magical and spiritual ends.

The fundamental idea of sex magic is intentionality, or the deliberate focus of sexual energy on particular objectives or wants. Sex magic encourages people to participate in sexual actions with a specific and intentional goal, in contrast to traditional sexual encounters where the focus may be exclusively on physical pleasure. This goal could be anything from spiritual awakening and fulfilling particular goals to personal empowerment and healing. To intensify the energy and intention underlying their urges, practitioners work to develop a heightened level of consciousness throughout the sexual act.

Reclaiming one's sexuality from social constraints and taboos is closely related to the idea of personal empowerment through sex magic. Throughout history, sexual expression has frequently been associated with shame or guilt due to cultural and religious restrictions, which has caused people to form complicated connections with their impulses. Sex magic encourages a deliberate and uninhibited exploration of one's sexuality, which defies these limitations. Through purposeful and thoughtful practice, people can peel back layers of guilt and shame and reclaim their sexual identity as a source of empowerment.

An essential component of using sex magic for self-empowerment is realizing the mind-body link. By encouraging people to be completely present in their bodies during sexual acts, the practice helps people develop a strong bond with their emotions and physical experiences. Emotional barriers, trauma from the past, and sluggish energy can all be released from the body through this embodiment. People can regain control over their bodies and sexuality through this process, opening the door to more uninhibited expression of desire and personal empowerment.

The use of breathwork, a feature shared by numerous spiritual practices, enhances the transforming capacity of sex magic even more. During sexual experiences, breathing that is conscious and rhythmic creates a link between the physical and energy realms. Through the expansion and circulation of sexual energy throughout the body, breathwork facilitates a feeling of fluidity and vigor in people. Intentional control over breath not only improves the experience overall but also makes it easier for sexual energy to be transformed for spiritual development and personal empowerment.

Transcending the egoic self and establishing connections with higher realms of awareness are vital components of the spiritual growth component of sex magic. Tantra views sexual energy as a potent means of reaching enlightenment on a spiritual level. Through specific disciplines like visualization, breathwork, and meditation, people can intentionally channel their sexual energy and experience expanded awareness and altered states of consciousness. In this framework, the combination of sexual and spiritual energy is understood as a means of gaining access to the universal source of consciousness and overcoming the limitations of the individual self.

Within the context of sex magic, meditation techniques enhance the spiritual aspect of the encounter. Meditation, which is frequently connected to quiet and introspection, can be easily incorporated into sexual rituals. When doing sex magic, partners may decide to intersperse silent meditation, visualization, or mantra chanting. These exercises increase consciousness, strengthen bonds between couples, and establish a sacred, purposeful environment for spiritual inquiry.

Sex magic has a powerful symbolic and ritual component that adds to its transformational power. The sexual act is given an additional layer of intention and significance through the use of symbols, sacred geometry, or particular rituals. Rituals can be as basic as setting up a holy area with candles and incense or as complex as adhering to a prewritten ritual that includes certain invocations. These symbolic components act as anchors for intentionality, assisting people in directing their concentration and energy toward the intended result—personal empowerment, healing, or spiritual connection, for example.

Sex magic can be studied within the dynamics of consensual and communicative partnerships rather than being limited to individual practices as a tool for spiritual development and personal empowerment. When two people are having sex magic together, they might create a space where both parties can explore and transform. The practice is made to be a cooperative and powerful experience for both parties by emphasizing permission, honest communication, and shared aims. Co-creating rituals, making shared intentions, and starting a spiritual and personal growth journey are all possible for couples.

Although sex magic can transform lives, it is crucial to approach the art with awareness and morality. Consent and communication are essential to ensure everyone is at ease and agrees with the practice's goals. To further their understanding and improve the safety of their explorations, individuals, and partners interested in sex magic may find it helpful to consult with seasoned practitioners, Tantric teachers, or spiritual mentors.

In conclusion, sex magic invites people to rediscover and investigate the transforming possibilities of their sexuality. It is a discipline at the nexus of spiritual development and personal empowerment. Sex magic, which has its roots in antiquated customs and has been modified by modern mystics, subverts social taboos and promotes the deliberate and free expression of desire. Through intentionality, awareness, breathwork, meditation, symbolism, and ritual, people can effectively harness the force of sexual energy to achieve both spiritual elevation and personal empowerment. When sex magic is used in voluntary relationships or alone, it becomes a sacred path of self-discovery.

CHAPTER VI

Exploring Boundaries and Consent

The importance of consent and communication in sex magic

Within the esoteric domain of sex magic, sexuality, which is frequently obscured by cultural taboos and societal restraints, goes through a transformation that is not found anywhere else. Utilizing the tremendous energy of sexuality for spiritual discovery, personal empowerment, and transformation, sex magic is a practice that has its origins in ancient traditions and is now being practiced by modern practitioners. Consent and communication emerge as important pillars within this holy and deliberate practice, establishing the ethical basis that ensures the safety, respect, and alignment of all persons involved. This practice is a sacred and intentional activity. Within the scope of this section, we will delve into the fundamental relevance of consent and communication in the practice of sex magic. We will investigate how these principles protect the well-being of individuals and encourage a peaceful exploration of the mystical possibilities of sexuality.

"Sex magic" refers to the practice of consciously employing sexual energy to bring about the manifestation of one's intentions, desires, or spiritual aspirations. Not only does the strength lie in the act itself, but it also lies in the intentional direction of this powerful force. The practitioners engage in sexual rituals with focused goals, merging the physical and metaphysical aspects of the act. This is done in the framework of personal empowerment and spiritual development. Therefore, consent and communication become vital components to guarantee that all parties agree on their aims, boundaries, and levels of comfort.

Through the application of the notion that the energy that is generated during sexual experiences is a transformational power, the practice of sex magic can function. To harness this energy in a manner that is both ethical and responsible, an essential component of any sex magic practice is consent. A clear and enthusiastic agreement to participate in particular acts, rituals, or goals is required to consider consent. Consent goes beyond merely acknowledging that one is participating in something. When it comes to the arena of sex magic, where intents and energies are purposefully directed, the requirement for explicit and continuing agreement is of the utmost importance to establish a place that is characterized by reliability and esteem.

In the context of sex magic, communication encompasses not only the expression of desires through verbalization but also the expression of boundaries, preferences, and goals. Communication that is both open and honest should take place between individuals or partners who are engaging in sex magic before the beginning of any sexual endeavor. Through this conversation, it is possible to investigate each person's comfort levels and desires, as well as any potential issues or restrictions. Via the promotion of open and honest communication, individuals can jointly create an environment that is emotionally and spiritually secure, which is favorable to the transforming experiences that are desired via the practice of sex magic.

The idea of affirmative consent, in which all participants voluntarily and voluntarily choose to participate in particular actions, is fundamental when it comes to the setting of sex magic. Sex magic rituals, in contrast to traditional sexual interactions, frequently entail purposeful practices, symbolism, and energetic labor that call for mutual understanding and consent between the participants. Practitioners can add a variety of varied components to their sexual encounters. These elements may include breathwork, imagery, or specialized rituals. By ensuring that all individuals involved are aware of and comfortable with the intended practices, clear communication helps reduce the likelihood of misunderstandings or discomfort occurring because of the practices.

When it comes to sex magic, consent is not a one-time agreement but rather a process that is continual and ever-changing. Individuals can experience shifts in their energies, emotions, or states of consciousness as the ritual process progresses. Maintaining open lines of communication makes it possible to conduct continuous check-ins, enabling participants to communicate any changes in their comfort level or experiences. This continual consent helps to cultivate an atmosphere of trust and attunement, ensuring that all those engaged feel empowered to convey their requirements and limits throughout the ritual.

In many cases, the techniques of sex magic incorporate aspects of vulnerability, intimacy, and profound introspection of the practitioner. When viewed in this light, clear communication transforms into a helpful instrument for navigating the emotional and energy landscapes that may emerge during the ritual. There is a possibility that practitioners will experience feelings, memories, or sensations that are unexpected. The capacity to interact openly with partners provides a container for the practitioner to explore and integrate these different experiences. A shared comprehension of these subtle characteristics is made possible by efficient communication, which extends beyond the physical world to include emotional and energetic dimensions. Consent encompasses more than just the material sphere.

The incorporation of communication and consent into sex magic is essential when it is performed within the context of a partnership that is of mutual consent. Establishing a foundation of trust, respect, and shared intentionality is necessary for individuals or couples who are engaging in sex magic together. It is possible to negotiate the complications of sex magic with more ease through the formation of partnerships that are built on excellent communication and mutual understanding. This will ensure that the practice becomes an experience that is collaborative and empowering for all individual participants.

Non-verbal clues and energetic attunement are also essential components in the practice of sex magic, in addition to verbal communication, which plays a less significant role. It is necessary for partners participating in rituals to be aware of one other's body language, subtle signals, and dynamic fluctuations in energy. The use of non-verbal communication acts as an additional layer of permission, allowing for a more nuanced knowledge of each participant's experience and comfort levels. It is essential to have the capacity to recognize subtle indications to strengthen the overall connection and guarantee that the practice will continue to be mutually entertaining and respectful.

Both consent and communication are essential components of sex magic, and they extend beyond the immediate ritual to include the phase of integration and the aftermath. Participants can experience a variety of feelings, insights, or alterations in their energetic state after engaging in sex magic practices. By participating in post-ritual talks, individuals can express their experiences, thoughts, and any new understandings they may have obtained throughout the ritual. This phase of communication contributes to the ongoing process of personal development and the integration of the transforming energies generated during the practice.

When it comes to sex magic, the ethical considerations of consent and communication extend to the possible impact on the larger community as well. Even though sex magic is a private and intimate activity, individuals have a responsibility to always keep in mind the potential repercussions that their acts may have within the more excellent framework of society. Practitioners need to take into consideration the ramifications of sharing their experiences or engaging in sex magic practices within groups or online platforms, particularly about privacy, consent, and ethics. To uphold the ethical values of the practice, it is vital to have open and honest communication regarding the limits of sharing and to protect the privacy of all people involved.

Understanding personal boundaries and negotiation in sexual rituals

In the arena of sexual rituals, a one-of-a-kind tapestry of investigation is revealed; it is a tapestry that digs into the esoteric and personal parts of the human experience. Personal limits and the ability to negotiate are two elements that are essential to the conduct of sexual rituals in a way that is both ethical and consensual. Understanding and respecting personal boundaries is critical to building a safe and empowering environment for all parties involved, regardless of whether the person's spiritual practices are rooted in old traditions, modern mysticism, or contemporary spiritual practices. This section aims to investigate the complex dynamics of personal boundaries in sexual rituals. Specifically, we will explore the significance of open communication, mutual agreement, and the ongoing negotiation of desires within the holy setting of these life-altering experiences.

The psychological, emotional, and physical restrictions individuals set up for themselves to safeguard their well-being are known as personal boundaries. These boundaries are fluid and specific to each individual. In the context of sexual rituals, it is necessary to acknowledge and respect personal limits to cultivate an atmosphere that is characterized by trust, safety, and respect. These rituals are performed by practitioners with a wide variety of goals in mind, ranging from promoting personal empowerment and healing to investigating spirituality. The ability to comprehend and negotiate one's boundaries becomes essential in ensuring that these encounters are ethical, consensual, and by the desires and degrees of comfort of all participants.

To conduct sexual rituals ethically, clear communication is vitally important. Participants must engage in open and honest conversation before beginning any ceremonial activity. This is done to develop mutual understanding and get permission. The purpose of this conversation is to construct a shared framework within which the sexual ritual can take place. This framework is created by discussing individual desires, boundaries, and objectives. The ability to communicate effectively acts as a compass, directing practitioners through the complexity of personal limits and providing a basis for the investigation of consensual relationships.

The practice of sexual rituals is inherently characterized by negotiation, which is a process that is both ongoing and dynamic. When individuals or partners engage in the voyage of sexual exploration, it is possible that their wants may change, that their limits will vary, and that they will gain new insights. Discussions and check-ins should be constant, and there should be a readiness to change as the event progresses. Effective negotiating requires all of these things. Maintaining this ongoing conversation ensures that all participants feel empowered to communicate their requirements, establish or modify limits, and genuinely navigate the ritual by their consent.

In the framework of sexual rituals, practitioners frequently include particular practices, forms of symbolism, or energetic work into the encounter. All parties concerned need to have a shared understanding and agree to negotiate the inclusion of these components successfully. As the guiding principle in deciding the scope and nature of the ritual, consent, when stated positively and explicitly, becomes the subject of consideration. Practitioners can negotiate the use of particular symbols, rituals, or purposeful practices to guarantee that all parties engaged are at ease and in agreement with the experience that is the intended outcome.

In sexual rituals, it is essential to have a well-rounded understanding of the various aspects of personal limits. Practitioners are required to traverse the physical, emotional, and energetic components of personal boundaries with delicacy and respect. Personal boundaries comprise all three different dimensions. The levels of comfort that are associated with touch, proximity, and particular activities are what constitute physical limits. The level of emotional closeness that participants are willing to explore and the sharing of emotions and vulnerabilities are all aspects that fall under the category of emotional limits. An attunement to the subtle dynamics at play is required to successfully navigate energetic boundaries, which involve the interchange and circulation of energy inside the ritual.

Conversations on aftercare and integration are included in negotiating personal limits, which go beyond the immediate ritual. Aftercare comprises the supportive practices and check-ins that take place after the ritual to guarantee the health and happiness of all those who participated in the ceremony. Practitioners can contribute to the continued development and comprehension of the transforming energies harnessed during the ritual by sharing their experiences, ideas, and comments through integrative conversations. To engage in sexual ritual activities that are ethical, it is necessary to negotiate the aftercare and integration process beforehand.

Consent, which serves as the foundation of sexual rituals that adhere to ethical standards, must be informed, enthusiastic, and continuing. Consent that is reported requires a thorough comprehension of the activities that will be carried out, the risks involved, and the intentions being held for the ritual. Practitioners need to be aware of the precise techniques involved and any potential emotional or energy experiences that may become apparent. A wholehearted and voluntary decision to participate in the ritual is what is meant by enthusiastic consent. This agreement ensures that all participants are freely and actively involved in the ritual. The concept of ongoing consent highlights the dynamic nature of the ritual by recognizing that participants may seek to change or renegotiate limits as the experience progresses.

Within the context of group sexual rituals, where numerous people come together to experience a shared transforming experience, it is essential to have clear communication and to negotiate personal boundaries. Because of the wide range of individual preferences, levels of comfort, and intents, it is necessary to commit more to open communication and permission in these situations. A collective understanding of the ethical implications surrounding personal boundaries is required for group rituals. This awareness should emphasize the necessity of communal agreements, assistance from facilitators, and a shared commitment to respect and consent.

Personal boundaries in sexual rituals are intricately connected to the idea of vulnerability, which encompasses both the psychological and emotional components of these boundaries. A common practice among participants is to put themselves in sensitive positions to investigate various elements of their minds, desires, and emotional territory. To successfully negotiate personal limits, it is essential to recognize and respect the vulnerability being discussed. Together with the participants, the facilitators are required to approach the experience with empathy and compassion, as well as an understanding of the sensitive nature of the journey that they are traveling together.

Certain sexual ritual practices may involve the concept of power exchange, as well as the idea of dominance and submission that is based on consent. Because this dynamic involves an intentional and mutually agreed-upon transfer of power between individuals, it necessitates an even more complex approach to the negotiation of personal boundaries. It is of the utmost importance to achieve clear communication on roles, expectations, and boundaries mutually agreed upon to guarantee that the power dynamic continues to be consensual, respectful, and within the comfort levels of all parties.

When it comes to sexual rituals, the ethical considerations of personal boundaries extend beyond the current experience to include the potential impact on the well-being of individuals from another perspective. When participating in the ritual, practitioners should be aware of the possible psychological, emotional, and energy impacts of the practice, and they should also take measures to assist each other's integration and well-being. In many cases, facilitators or practitioners with extensive expertise play a significant role in helping participants through the ethical aspects of the practice and providing resources for continued support.

In conclusion, the essential principles of recognizing, negotiating, and respecting personal limits are the foundation upon which the ethical practice of sexual rituals is built. A container for consensual exploration is created when there is clear communication between all parties involved. This container ensures that all participants actively engage in a shared understanding of their degree of comfort, desires, and objectives. Given the fluid nature of personal boundaries in sexual rituals, it is necessary to engage in continuous negotiation, demonstrate adaptation, and demonstrate a commitment to mutual respect. By adhering to these ethical norms, sexual rituals have the potential to become experiences that are transforming and uplifting. They can also stimulate personal development, spiritual exploration, and a journey of consensual self-discovery that is shared by the parties involved.

Techniques for establishing trust and creating a safe space for exploration

Regarding personal development, spiritual discovery, and intimate relationships, trust is the foundation upon which transformative experiences are constructed. Establishing a secure environment is of the utmost importance for persons who wish to dive into vulnerable portions of themselves, regardless of whether the setting is therapy, spiritual practices, or the exploration of consensual topics. The purpose of this section is to investigate a variety of approaches to developing trust and cultivating a secure environment for inquiry. The author acknowledges the significant influence that these practices may have on promoting growth, connection, and the unfolding of one's inner journey.

Trust, which can be described as the reliance on the honesty, power, and capability of a person or object, is the foundation upon which every significant and transformational investigation is built. Within the framework of therapeutic interactions, establishing trust is a fundamental component that grants individuals the opportunity to disclose their most profound concerns, traumatic experiences, and goals. Beginning with the development of clear boundaries and ethical principles, therapists utilize a variety of approaches to establish and strengthen trust in their interactions with clients. The framework that therapists construct for their clients allows them to feel safe enough to explore their inner landscapes. This framework is created by honest communication concerning the therapeutic process, confidentiality, and mutual expectations.

When it comes to fostering trust in interpersonal relationships, active listening is a powerful method utilized not only in therapeutic settings but also in various communication settings. Demonstrating a profound regard for the individual's singular experiences and points of view can be conveyed through careful listening that is free from judgment and interruption. The practice of reflective listening, in which the listener paraphrases or summarizes what the speaker has revealed, helps to improve understanding and validates the speaker's feelings. This practice is utilized in the process of creating a safe place. Through the demonstration of a genuine interest in the other person's story and a dedication to comprehending their subjective world, this method contributes to the development of trust within the relationship.

Building and sustaining trust requires several factors, one of which is consistency. It is essential to maintain consistent behavior and predictable reactions to foster a sense of safety, whether in the context of personal ties, mentorship, or therapeutic interactions. Individuals can experience a sense of security and stability when they can anticipate the behaviors and activities of other people. It is common practice for therapists and facilitators to highlight the significance of maintaining regular attendance, timeliness, and adherence to agreements to establish an atmosphere where clients feel they are solidly supported regarding their investigations.

There is a considerable correlation between the creation of trust and the disclosure of information regarding therapeutic or exploratory procedures. It is beneficial for those participating in transformational experiences or therapy to have a clear awareness of the processes, goals, and potential problems linked with the process. Through the process of demystifying the investigation and openly explaining the outcomes sought, therapists can establish an atmosphere in which clients can make decisions based on accurate information and actively engage in their own personal growth journey. By eliminating uncertainty and promoting cooperative collaboration, this transparency results in the development of trust.

Recognizing and respecting individuals' autonomy is another component of creating a secure environment for free exploration. When clients or participants can make decisions regarding the pace, depth, and direction of their investigation, it results in an increased sense of agency. When working with clients in therapeutic settings, therapists work together with clients to establish goals and investigate themes that align with the client's priorities and degrees of comfort. By emphasizing the individual's autonomy and allowing them to take control of their journey, this collaborative approach helps to cultivate trust.

Establishing rituals or routines contributes to a sense of safety and predictability during the exploration process. Whether they entail the beginning or finish of a session, the use of certain symbols, or the repetition of comfortable activities, rituals create an ordered and familiar environment. Individuals can navigate the sometimes uncertain terrain of personal inquiry with greater ease when engaging in these rituals because they signify safety and create a sense of continuity. Through the use of these rituals, therapists and facilitators help to the creation of an exploration space that is both reassuring and safe.

When creating a safe environment for inquiry, using trauma-informed methods is essential. This is especially true when individuals may be carrying past scars or sensitivities. Psychotherapists and facilitators who have received training in trauma-informed techniques are aware of the possible impact that persons' previous traumatic experiences may have on their current experiences. To ensure that clients feel valued and supported while they traverse their inner landscapes, these professionals prioritize safety, encourage empowerment, and emphasize choice during the exploration process.

Establishing trust and creating a secure environment for investigation goes beyond the limitations of verbal communication. When it comes to feelings of empathy, attunement, and emotional safety, non-verbal clues, such as body language and facial expressions, play a crucial part in transmitting these emotions. To ensure that they can convey feelings of warmth, openness, and understanding through their demeanor, therapists and facilitators frequently participate in training programs designed to strengthen their non-verbal communication abilities. Through the alignment of verbal and non-verbal communication, experts can enhance the overall sense of trust and safety within the exploration area.

The values of trust and safety continue to be of the

utmost importance in the consensual exploration that takes place inside intimate partnerships. It is beneficial for partners interested in exploring new activities or deepening their connection to communicate openly and honestly about their desires, boundaries, and expectations related to the relationship. Establishing mutual consent becomes essential, highlighting the significance of enthusiastic agreement to participate in particular activities. This consent is not static; it develops throughout the exploration process, necessitating continual discussion and negotiation to guarantee that all persons involved feel respected and at ease.

Negotiating explicit agreements and establishing

boundaries are also components of exploring with consent. Partners participating in experiences that are either intimate or transformative ought to have an open conversation about their preferences, limits, and expectations. Through negotiation, individuals can communicate their degrees of comfort, establish boundaries, and align themselves on the shared objectives of their inquiry. Regular check-ins and continued communication throughout the exploration process ensure that both partners remain attuned to each other's needs and maintain a supportive and consensual environment.

Within the realm of consensual exploration, using safe

phrases or signals is a widely acknowledged and utilized strategy. This is especially true in activities involving power dynamics or components of dominance and submission. Individuals can communicate their discomfort or the desire to cease the inquiry in a clear and unambiguous way when they utilize safe phrases. By using safe words, one can create a structured and courteous setting for conducting consensual exploration. This environment highlights the significance of continual consent and continuing communication.

Building trust and safety is considerably aided by disseminating information and understanding regarding the exploration process. It is beneficial for partners participating in transformative experiences to have a shared awareness of the methods, practices, and potential difficulties related to their investigation. By having this shared understanding, both parties can ensure that they are fully educated, that they are prepared for the exploration, and that they can actively participate in building a safe and non-threatening environment for their journey.

It is essential for persons who are either engaging in or guiding transformative exploration to commit to continual education and self-awareness. The knowledge and abilities of professionals in therapeutic or facilitation roles are constantly being updated, particularly in areas associated with trauma-informed practices, consent, and ethical exploration. This commitment guarantees that facilitators will be able to adjust to the ever-changing requirements of individuals and establish a conducive environment that emphasizes trust, respect, and safety.

In conclusion, the methods that aim to generate trust and create a secure environment for inquiry are varied and depend on the context in which they are implemented. Whether it be in the context of therapeutic settings, consensual intimate relationships, or spiritual practices, the cornerstone of a safe exploration environment is comprised of the values of clear communication, transparency, respect for autonomy, and trauma-informed techniques.

Navigating ethical considerations and potential challenges in sex magic practices

Sex magic is a technique that is both esoteric and mystical, and it bridges the gap between sexuality and spirituality. It can bring about significant inward transformation and self-discovery. In the process of persons embarking on the journey of adding sex magic into their spiritual practices, ethical issues transform into the most critical factor. A mindful and conscientious approach is required to guarantee that practitioners negotiate consent, intentionality, and personal boundaries with respect and ethical integrity. This is because the union of sexuality and spirituality requires a mindful and concerned attitude. This section investigates the ethical considerations that are inherent in the practices of sex magic. It sheds light on potential obstacles and offers insights into how to nurture a responsible and empowered engagement with this transformational art form.

Consent is the principle that stands at the center of the ethical considerations that are involved in the practice of sex magic. When compared to traditional sexual interactions, sex magic is characterized by the deliberate and ceremonial utilization of sexual energy for the sake of spiritual advancement. Because of the consensual nature of these activities, it is necessary for all persons involved to have open lines of communication and reach a consensus with one another. Within the realm of sex magic, consent encompasses more than only acknowledging one's participation; rather, it entails an unambiguous and enthusiastic consent to participate in particular rites, intentions, or practices. It is the responsibility of practitioners to ensure that all those involved are fully aware, willing, and actively participating in the joint exploration. This will ultimately help to cultivate an atmosphere of trust and respect.

When it comes to sex magic techniques, another important ethical aspect is the importance of being transparent about intentions and expectations. It is essential for people who engage in these activities to talk honestly about their objectives, wants, and how they intend to use their sexual energy. It is essential to maintain transparency to guarantee that all participants agree with the primary aim of the ritual. This is true regardless of whether the focus is on personal empowerment, healing, or spiritual connection. The practitioners can manage the transforming parts of sex magic with clarity and purpose as a result of this openness, which generates a shared understanding and strengthens the consensual nature of the encounter.

In the realm of sex magic activities, one of the most important ethical considerations is respect for personal boundaries. Because these rituals are deliberate and energetic, they can elicit profound feelings, vulnerabilities, or memories. It is essential for practitioners to demonstrate sensitivity to each participant's personal boundaries and to prioritize the participants' mental and physical health. By maintaining open lines of communication on comfort levels, potential triggers, and the desire to investigate particular topics, it is possible to guarantee that all parties involved feel safe and valued. It is possible to contribute to the ethical practice of sex magic by cultivating an atmosphere that respects and honors personal limits. This helps to prevent potential harm and promotes an experience that is both consensual and empowering to the individual.

To successfully navigate the ethical landscape of sex magic practices, it is necessary to take into consideration power dynamics and the possibility of imbalances occurring inside the ritual. It is essential for participants to consciously and voluntarily transfer power to one another to engage in power exchange, which is a common component of several sex magic techniques. Practitioners who take on dominating or submissive positions should ensure that all people engaged in the situation negotiate, make explicit, and agree upon the power dynamics. In the field of ethics, practitioners acknowledge the significance of maintaining open lines of communication, monitoring power dynamics, and ensuring that all individuals feel respected and empowered within their appropriate responsibilities.

When it comes to sex magic practices, cultural sensitivity is an essential ethical issue, mainly when drawing inspiration from a variety of spiritual or esoteric traditions. It is possible to avoid misrepresenting or appropriating religious aspects by respecting the cultural backgrounds, symbols, and rituals one is familiar with. It is essential for practitioners to approach the incorporation of cultural aspects with mindfulness, to gain an understanding of and respect for the origins and meanings behind them. To ensure that sex magic practices are not only respectful but also contribute to the preservation and appreciation of a wide variety of cultural manifestations, ethical engagement with cultural factors is essential.

One other difficulty associated with the practice of sex magic is the possibility of spiritual bypassing. This refers to the situation in which individuals engage in spiritual practices, such as sex magic, to avoid confronting unsolved psychological complications or emotional concerns. Ethical practitioners are aware of blending spiritual experiences with psychological well-being when they practice. They do not view sex magic as a replacement for addressing the underlying problems; instead, they view it as a supplement to personal development and healing experiences. It is essential for practitioners to be aware of the possibility of spiritual bypassing and to maintain their dedication to holistic well-being. When necessary, they should seek the assistance of professionals to navigate psychological problems successfully.

The combination of sex magic and personal relationships brings about extra ethical considerations to be taken into account. An open line of communication, the negotiation of wants, and mutual agreement should be the top priorities for practitioners in the context of consensual partnerships. Because of the intricacies of intimate relationships, it is necessary to have a heightened awareness of the emotional and relational factors involved. Ethical practitioners are aware of the possible impact that sex magic can have on the dynamics of a relationship and engage in continuous communication to guarantee that both parties have a sense of respect and support in their individual and shared journeys.

When it comes to sex magic practices, it is essential to address any issues that are associated with gender dynamics and power imbalances. The method in which sex magical rituals are approached might be influenced by the historical context of gender inequality and the power relations that exist within society. Ethical practitioners work toward creating rituals that are inclusive and empowering and free from the reinforcement of harmful stereotypes and shifts in power dynamics. Within the context of the ceremony, making conscious attempts to foster equality, communication, and mutual respect are all factors that lead to an ethical and empowering practice of sex magic.

Within the realm of sex magic activities, there is a substantial ethical concern regarding the possibility of compulsion or manipulation. It is essential for practitioners to be aware of the dynamics currently taking place within the ritual and to make sure that all participants participate voluntarily and enthusiastically. Ethical practitioners make it a point to intentionally seek out and eradicate any components of coercion. Hence, they respect the autonomy of individuals and avoid any pressure or manipulation that could weaken the sense of consent associated with the experience. Participants should feel empowered to communicate their boundaries without fear of penalties, and all participants should freely grant permission.

When it comes to sex magic practices, confidentiality, and privacy are of the utmost importance from an ethical standpoint. This is especially true when practitioners perform rituals within communities or group settings. To foster a culture of trust and respect, it is essential to respect the privacy of the individuals involved, to maintain confidentiality regarding personal experiences, and to obtain consent before revealing facts. Ethical practitioners place a high priority on maintaining the secrecy of participants, thereby establishing an atmosphere where individuals can freely explore without the expectation that their experiences will be disclosed without their agreement.

To summarise, the process of navigating ethical considerations in sex magic practices is an ongoing and ever-changing process that necessitates mindfulness, communication, and a dedication to mutual respect. Ethical practitioners are required to promote clear communication, transparency, and the understanding of personal limits because of the consensual and intentional nature of sex magic. However, this is only sometimes the case. The practitioners of sex magic contribute to developing ethical and powerful practices by developing a culture of respect for cultural sensitivities, addressing power relations, and encouraging equality within rituals. In the process of individuals exploring the transforming possibilities of sexuality and spirituality, an ethical foundation assures that the path is one of self-discovery, progress, and empowerment via the voluntary participation of the in

CHAPTER VII

Integrating Sex Magic into Daily Life

Bringing sex magic into everyday experiences and relationships

Many people view sex magic, a mystical discipline that unites spirituality and sensuality, as a holy and arcane endeavor. Sex magic's transformative power, however, need not be limited to ceremonial environments or unique occasions; it may be incorporated into regular interactions and relationships. This section delves into the practice of infusing sex magic into everyday situations, emphasizing the ways that purposeful and deliberate sexuality may enhance life, strengthen bonds, and foster individual and interpersonal development.

Sex magic is fundamentally about using sexual energy for transformation purposefully and ceremonially. The fundamental component of sex magic is the deliberate focus of sexual energy on specific purposes or objectives, even though ancient techniques may involve complex rituals, symbols, and ceremonies. An essential element in integrating sex magic into regular encounters is realizing that sexual energy is a powerful force that penetrates every part of existence. People can intentionally bring intentionality and awareness into their daily interactions and relationships by comprehending and accepting this essential component.

A fundamental component of incorporating sex magic into regular experiences is communication. It is essential to have direct and honest conversations with oneself and, if appropriate, a partner. To investigate their goals, wants, and the place of sexuality in their everyday lives, people can exercise introspection. A closer relationship with one's sexual energy and its capacity for transformation can be fostered through reflective writing, meditation, or just making time for self-examination. As a result of open communication between partners regarding intents, aims, and desires, sex magic can become a cooperative and mutually enhancing activity in relationships.

Practicing mindfulness, which is based on being present at the moment, is a great way to incorporate sex magic into regular encounters. People can increase their awareness of the feelings, energies, and sensations that are present during sexual experiences by practicing mindfulness. Being mindful while doing daily tasks or spending a private moment with a significant other enables people to access the transformational power of sexual energy. A closer relationship with the current moment and the energy transferred within it is fostered by mindfulness, which also opens the door to enhanced sensory experiences.

Routines and rituals provide a rich environment for integrating sex magic into daily life. Routines in the morning or evening, such as taking a shower, getting ready for the day, or relaxing before bed, can be transformed into conscious times to focus on releasing sexual energy. People can transform these routines from ordinary duties into holy rituals by bringing consciousness into them. During these daily rituals, subtle yet effective strategies to channel and direct sexual energy toward personal purposes or goals include visualization, breathwork, or brief periods of concentration.

The specificity and clarity of one's wants are what give intentionality in sex magic its strength. People might make intentions for the day, the week, or specific activities when incorporating sex magic into ordinary life. These goals can include developing stronger interpersonal relationships, creative expression, and self-empowerment. For instance, people can take a moment to create an intention for concentration, productivity, and creative inspiration before beginning a task at work. This allows sexual energy to bring vigor and purpose to the action.

Relationships that involve shared experiences offer a wealth of opportunities to incorporate sex magic into everyday life. Co-creating intentions for their relationship allows partners to explore strategies to improve communication, strengthen their bond, and work through obstacles as a team. Commonplace pursuits like cooking, gardening, or even working out together can be designated areas for directing sexual energy toward one another's objectives. Couples can try subtle practices like eye gazing, synchronized breathwork, or other techniques to build a sense of intentionality and connection during these activities.

Bringing sex magic into daily life naturally leads to an exploration of sensuality in ordinary encounters. Indulging all of the senses and appreciating the sights, sounds, textures, and scents of the present is what it means to be sensual. When having a meal, going for a walk outdoors, or having a private moment with a significant other, people can deliberately use their senses to enhance the experience. In addition to making daily tasks more enjoyable, this increased sensuality also provides a means of establishing a connection with the sensual qualities of sexual energy.

When researching sex magic, including breathwork into daily life takes on a transforming quality. Breath acts as a link between the physical and energetic realms and is closely associated with sexual energy. People can engage in mindful breathing throughout the day by paying attention to their breaths, both in and out. This straightforward yet effective technique encourages a sense of vitality, presence, and inner self-connection by circulating and amplifying sexual energy. During intimate moments, partners might synchronize their breathing, strengthening their bond.

Another way to add sex magic into regular encounters is to partake in artistic endeavors. Since creativity and sexual energy are manifestations of life force energy, they have a close relationship. Through writing, art, or even just solving problems in daily life, people can purposefully inject sexual energy into their creative processes. By using the transforming power of sexual energy to fuel their creative activities, people can use intentional creativity as a means of self-expression and empowerment.

Attempting to include sex magic in regular experiences

can be difficult, particularly in a society that frequently compartmentalizes sexuality. A dedication to self-discovery and accepting one's passions is necessary to overcome inhibitions and societal conditioning. It is essential to have a loving and nonjudgmental attitude toward oneself. Additionally, navigating shared experiences and aspirations requires efficient communication with partners, if relevant. Practitioners can run into opposition or doubt, but the secret is to keep investigating and modifying the integration of sex magic in a way that feels true to oneself and compatible with one's ideals.

Setting boundaries is essential when integrating sex

magic into regular interactions. Although the exercise promotes transparency and inquiry, honoring one's

Setting limits and comfort zones is crucial. To maintain

consent and empower others, people should be aware of their needs and express them to partners clearly and concisely. By setting limits within the practice, people can navigate the transforming power of sexual energy in a way that is consistent with their development journey and ideals.

Incorporating sex magic into regular encounters raises

ethical questions about mutual empowerment, consent, and respect. One's own or other people's autonomy or well-being should never be violated intentionally. Practitioners should be aware of power dynamics to ensure that shared experiences within partnerships are consensual and mutually beneficial. When integrating sex magic, transparency, and open communication become moral rules that promote a respectful and trusting atmosphere.

Conclusively, integrating sex magic into regular encounters and relationships is a purposeful and dynamic activity that can foster personal and interpersonal development. People can access the transformational power of sexual energy by bringing conscious knowledge and intentionality into daily activities, shared moments, and secret rituals. Accepting the sacredness of sexuality in day-to-day living cultivates a feeling of purpose, vigor, and connection. The integration of sex magic becomes a voyage of self-discovery, empowerment, and the revelation that the sacred and the commonplace are interwoven parts of a comprehensive human experience, whether through mindfulness, intention setting, or engaging the senses.

Incorporating sexual energy into creative pursuits and personal goals

Every person possesses sexual energy, a vital life force that can go well beyond its conventional connotations. Beyond its function in closeness, sexual energy can be captured and directed toward personal objectives and artistic endeavors. To shed light on how people might intentionally integrate this powerful force to support their creative endeavors and accomplish transformative personal goals, this section examines the complex relationship between sexual energy, creativity, and personal growth.

Many civilizations and spiritual traditions have long held the belief that sexual energy and creativity are intertwined. Many belief systems acknowledge that the life force energy that nourishes creativity and vigor is also the same force that causes sexual desire. Comprehending and accepting this association lays the groundwork for intentionally integrating sexual energy into artistic endeavors. When combined with the transformational power of sexual energy, creativity—whether represented through creative efforts, problem-solving, or new thinking—becomes a dynamic process.

Being conscious is essential when integrating sexual energy into artistic endeavors. By practicing mindfulness, one can develop an acute awareness of the here and now and pay attention to any new feelings, ideas, or sensations that surface. People can access the sensory and energetic components of sexual energy by cultivating a careful awareness of the experience. Increased sensitivity to one's power fosters a stronger connection to the source of inspiration, which opens the door to unleashing the creative potential within.

One of the most effective methods for directing sexual energy toward artistic undertakings is breathwork. Breath links the physical and energetic domains since it is closely associated with the rise and fall of sexual energy. Intentional and conscious breathwork energizes and circulates sexual energy throughout the body, bringing vitality and opening up a conduit for expression. People who practice breathwork, whether it is through deep belly breathing or rhythmic patterns, become more adept at guiding and controlling the flow of their sexual energy and establishing its foundation in the creative process.

Using sexual energy in artistic endeavors transforms visualization into a transforming technique. One way to channel this energy toward creative endeavors is to visualize the flow and movement of energy inside the body, especially in the sacral and root chakras connected to sexuality. One way to visualize is to picture the bright, pulsating energy, see it rising through the body, and imagine it flowing into the chosen creative project. By design, this depiction establishes a mutually beneficial interaction between artistic expression and sexual energy.

Incorporating sexual energy into creative rituals provides a disciplined way to intentionally bring creativity into everyday life. By creating a regular and deliberate framework, people can set the stage for channeling sexual energy, whether through morning routines, designated creative areas, or pre-creative rituals. These rituals, which might involve exercises like self-massage, breathwork, or meditation, foster an atmosphere that allows sexual energy to flow and express itself during the creative process freely.

Accepting that sexual energy is cyclical is in line with the ups and downs of creative inspiration. Individuals can respect the rhythm of their creative and energetic phases when they recognize that sexual energy follows natural cycles, just like creativity does. People who are experiencing high levels of sexual arousal may discover that they are more drawn to artistic endeavors. On the other hand, recognizing that periods of low energy demand relaxation and renewal guarantees a comprehensive and long-term strategy for both creative and sexual practices.

When it comes to artistic expression, people can experiment with incorporating sexual energy into many kinds of creativity. The expression of sexual energy can be effectively channeled through writing, painting, music, and dance. Artists can bring the vitality and raw authenticity of sexual energy into their work by using creative vision and conscious mindfulness. The unadulterated communication of the artist's inner life force through artistic expression establishes a unique and potent bond between the artist and the listener.

The transforming power of sexual energy can be directed toward self-improvement and goal achievement in addition to artistic pursuits. Intention, drive, and persistence interact dynamically when creating and pursuing personal goals. Through intentionally focusing sexual energy on these objectives, people can become more motivated, access a source of energy, and develop the grit required to overcome obstacles. The deliberate balancing of sexual energy with individual goals catalyzes empowerment and self-discovery.

Clarity of intention is essential when integrating sexual energy into personal objectives. As with personal goals, intentions are the driving force behind sexual behaviors. People can clearly state their objectives and give them the vigor and purpose of their sexual life force. This alignment allows people to pursue their goals with passion and purpose, creating a harmonious synergy between their inner aspirations and desired outcomes.

A more profound comprehension of one's desires and motives is fostered by mindful awareness of the relationship between sexual energy and personal objectives. People might investigate the emotional and energetic aspects of their goals, realizing that sexual energy can be the impetus for their desires. A more all-encompassing approach to personal development, where the path is imbued with a sense of life, purpose, and a real connection to one's inner desires, is built upon this self-awareness.

Integrating sexual energy into one's goals requires the use of grounding and balancing activities. Because sexual energy is so vital and dynamic, it might be necessary to use grounding techniques to maintain focus and stability. Engaging in activities like mindfulness exercises, nature walks, or meditation can assist people in keeping their equilibrium and avert the possibility of dispersed energy. By establishing a solid base, grounding techniques enable people to utilize the intensity of sexual energy for long-term productivity and focus on their objectives.

The ethical implications of integrating sexual energy into artistic endeavors and individual objectives center on self-awareness, permission, and respect. People should be aware of their comfort zones and limits to make sure that using sexual energy purposefully is consistent with their personal development goals and ideals. Navigating the ethical aspects of these behaviors requires open discussion with oneself and, if relevant, with partners. An honest and powerful integration of sexual energy into creative and personal development is facilitated by transparency, respect for personal limits, and a persistent dedication to self-discovery.

People who want to incorporate their sexual energy into their artistic endeavors and personal objectives may face difficulties, particularly in societies where there are still taboos or stigmas associated with sexuality. Dedication to self-exploration and a nonjudgmental attitude toward one's aspirations are necessary to overcome personal inhibitions and societal indoctrination. Navigating everyday experiences and intentions requires effective communication with partners, if relevant. The secret is to keep investigating and modifying the integration of sexual energy in a way that feels true to oneself and in line with personal ideals, even when practitioners may run against opposition or skepticism.

To sum up, bringing sexual energy into artistic endeavors and personal objectives is a dynamic and deliberate discipline with the potential for significant change. By acknowledging the inherent link between sexual energy, creativity, and personal development, people can access a reservoir of vigor, passion, and genuine expression. The integration of sexual energy becomes a voyage of self-discovery, empowerment, and the awareness that the transforming potential of sexuality extends well beyond its conventional confines, whether through mindfulness, breathwork, visualization, or deliberate rituals.

CONCLUSION

Desire Unleashed: Examining Sex Magic for Healing and Connection" takes readers on a life-changing expedition into the domains of spiritual power and intimacy. The book offers a distinctive viewpoint on the critical relationship between sexuality and spirituality by deftly tying together the strands of desire, magic, and healing. The author guides readers through the unexplored realm of sex magic with perceptive investigation and helpful advice, offering a way to enhance physical connections and harness spiritual energy for healing.

The book explores the complex aspects of desire and highlights how it can be a strong motivator for both individual and group development. It encourages readers to accept their impulses without judgment and to see them as doors leading to spirituality and self-discovery. By incorporating rituals and holy practices, the author reveals a means to reach a higher state of awareness, allowing people to access the spiritual aspect of their relationships.

Moreover, "Desire Unleashed" highlights the therapeutic qualities of sex magic, presenting it as a transforming instrument for both physical and mental health. The author skillfully blends traditional knowledge with contemporary understanding to offer a comprehensive view of sexuality that goes beyond social norms and promotes a more in-depth understanding of the self.

This e-book offers a provocative and inspirational roadmap for anyone looking for a deep link between spirituality, healing, and desire. It presents a thorough examination of sex magic as a way to establish spiritual intimacy and unleash inner power, challenging conventional views on sexuality. "Desire Unleashed" provides a transformative path towards connection, healing, and the unleashing of inner desires, serving as a lighthouse for people seeking a harmonious synthesis of their physical and spiritual identities.

Thank you for buying and reading/ listening to our book. If you found this book useful/ helpful please take a few minutes and leave a review on the platform where you purchased our book. Your feedback matters greatly to us.